Foreword

WHEN I FIRST MET CODY HOLMES it was on his ranch in the late fall with winter approaching. We took a walk out on his ranch with a group of visitors. The first thing you noticed was that he had not clipped off his pastures like his neighbors. His neighbor's pastures looked as if you had taken a vacuum cleaner and sucked every bit of forage off of them, leaving bare soil exposed. From a distance Cody's pasture looked rough, with weeds and some brambles growing in it.

On closer inspection all you could see was a massive sward of clovers, grasses and forbs. This is poor soil folks, very thin and rocky. It was hard to believe the amount of quality forage that Cody was growing through nothing but good grazing management. By resisting the pressure that most people feel to mow pastures to make them look pretty, Cody had stored enough forage to winter his cows with limited hay. I see it every day in the fall, folks clipping their pastures to make them look pretty, then feeding hay all winter long.

This is just one example of Cody's superb management program. He later took me out to another pasture that had 400 cow/

calf pairs grazing through it. The pasture was covered with oak sprouts. To the outsider, it looked awful, but the cows were grazing everything — and were fat! Cody was using what nature gave him and was working with it. Most folks would have gone bankrupt battling it with chemical sprays, brush hogging, etc. Cody's cows were living well off of what was there and were not complaining about it. This is another fine example of using what you have and working with it to make a profit.

One of the principles that Cody firmly believes in is that the cow has to work for you, not you working for the cow. In today's cow herds this practice is not adhered to very well. In this book, Cody will go over the processes required for, and selection of the right kind of cow for, a profitable cow herd. You simply cannot make excuses for your cows; either they perform in your environment with no added inputs, or they go to town. Cody does not get married to his cows. This is crucial in selecting for a profitable cow herd.

In today's fast-paced lifestyle it is easy to become so busy that you have no quality time to think. We get so busy putting out daily fires that we are constantly chasing our own tails. Cody is convinced that we all need time just to sit down and think. I know personally that I can make much better decisions when my mind is at ease and not distracted by daily concerns. In this book Cody covers the "time to think" period that every livestock operation should make routine.

One of the items that we all normally fall short on is keeping track of financials during the year. Cody covers this in detail as well. Where are you spending your money? What is the profit driver on your farm? What is your weak link? If you don't know, it is impossible to address a plan of action. This process is what separates the profitable ranches from the hobby ranches.

Another false belief that is being taught today is that you cannot grow grass without adding all of the proper soil amendments. This is simply not true. Cody explains the methods he uses to grow grass and build the soil using livestock as the primary tool. This is one of our *unfair advantages*. By using animals that have a rumen filled with microbes we can heal bankrupt soils and weak grass stands. It is extremely rewarding to turn a bankrupt soil bank around by using mob grazing. The cattle trample litter, break soil capping, plant seeds, and inoculate the soil with microbes with each grazing rotation. Cody will explain the methods he uses to do this.

Cody is one of the few ranchers that is making 100% of his income off his ranch. There is no town job to supplement his income. This makes him very conscious of every decision that he makes on his ranch. When Cody makes a mistake, there is no safety-net town job to fall back on. I believe that Cody is one of the most cost-conscious ranchers that I have ever met. This book covers his philosophy in his daily ranching. You are in for a rare treat. Find some idle time and sit back somewhere you can truly absorb everything Cody covers in this book. I promise it will make your operation, soils and livestock much more sustainable, and your life will be more enjoyable as well.

If you want to move your ranching operation into the profit column, I believe the knowledge that Cody shares with you in this book will put you on the right path. Cody and I come from a similar background. I grew up poor as well. Nobody knew what was in my heart. I had a dream and goal from a very young age of owning my own ranch. No one on earth can deprive you of your dream. If you have a love of ranching and living in the country, this book will cover the most profitable way of getting there. I believe Cody's book can turn your dreams into reality! Good grazing to everyone and may your grasses always be tall and green.

Greg Judy
Clark, Missouri
October 2010

Introduction

WHY DOES THERE SEEM TO BE so few people who are able to make a good living on their farms and ranches? Part of the answer could be that those who succeed have the intention to do so from the beginning. Rather than following trends in the industry and chasing market fluctuations, there is a consistency in their operations. I see an almost simplistic approach in their business plan. It is very true that one family ranch can feed thousands of people with a single calf crop, utilizing forage that has very little other use, raised on generally less sought-after countryside.

Most of us cattlemen are proud of our production and the high quality of human food stuffs resulting. There are many more who have desired to make a living in the cattle industry, but have not fared so well. I believe I have discovered the reasons behind most of these hard-working men and women not being able to fulfill their dreams in the cattle industry. I was one of these cattlemen who struggled for the better part of my career in cattle with very little success until I found the golden nugget.

Almost from the beginning of our American heritage has the concept of free ranges and cattle barons and horses running across the prairie have we Americans dreamed of such ideas. Less grandiose imaginations conjured up the serene picture of raising a family in a remote area working with livestock and living off the land. I believe these ideas are planted in our collective imaginations by heritage and destiny — allowing us more fortunate souls to carry the burden of feeding the mass of city dwellers. Even now in the 21st century when range cattle are the same as extinct and raising a family on the Ponderosa seems to be for the wealthy, there are plenty like myself and many of my closest friends who continue to make the effort.

Yes, I am proud that I can feed more people than most other ranchers in the world. I am quite confident that my grasslands are more productive and useful for the good of mankind than before my existence. I also enjoy raising a family in a semi-secluded environment. My dream comes true when I ride horseback through a group of fall-calving cows as they are about two-thirds through calving. Nothing compares to the feeling when the fall leaves have turned into a beautiful array of orange, yellow and red and a light jacket feels good. The grass is still green and lush from the cool temperatures and the creek is trickling with clean runoff from the warm fall rains. The cows are fat and the calves are playful with each other and I can't hear any traffic, cell phones, or high interest rates. This day is what keeps me in the cow business. If you could be right here at the right time I believe that you too would forego what the city and secure employment has to offer. For if this day does not keep you motivated to be in this business, nothing else imaginable could.

I was raised in an agricultural era and environment that emphasized and practiced hard work. It was hard work that can create realities that started out as mere dreams. Hard work begins with planning, all too often the forgotten tool of choice. When a person is born poor, like I was, it is the ability to keep dreaming that fuels the engine that keeps you heading toward a goal. If one is taught at an early age to not be afraid of hard work, if nothing else, the hard work can help occupy one's time while he approaches the sometimes never ending task of accomplishing some of those dreams. If it is certainly the hard work that does make your dreams come true, why is it that so many hard-working fellows and ladies don't always see their dreams through to fruition? I believe that hard work comes in more forms than just sweating at the brow. Having the ability to not accept failure or better yet, not accepting that falling down occasionally or regularly is any indication that you are not still heading towards the goal you dreamed of. In other words, we must never ever quit trying. If we are willing to work hard — and that does include sweating at the brow — and have a determination that absolutely no one else can puncture, we can make steps in the right direction to reach that dream. While we are on this journey, which I believe is actually the best part of this dream, we will learn how to utilize our strength originating from the ability to physically work hard, and let it manifest into works of wisdom and better decision making. If we see many others failing while a few individuals are succeeding at the same dream, we must ask ourselves at some point in time whether the failures are inherent with the subject or personally inflicted. I contend that in most cases I have caused most of my own problems.

After breathing on this earth now for more than 50 years and living my dream of raising cattle, I can see that very few of my purveyors, suppliers, government and university specialists, and other so-called experts in the various fields of agriculture ever really had my best interest at heart. I was working so hard most of the time that I took only the time required to assume the solutions and proposals they offered were helping me reach my dream. I also made the wrong assumption that all those in authoritative positions had mostly correct answers. It is by no fault of their actions that their solutions were incorrect. Their solutions were correct as far as they were concerned and as far as their education could take them. Their main objective was to work toward their goals, which was a basic need to sell one more widget, produce one more gadget, market one more bag of something in order to meet their or their bosses' or organization's objectives. This willingness to support oneself and work in a manner to do so is what minimizes the length of our soup lines and keeps the number of free riders at bay.

Just as building fences is hard work and so very important to the business of ranching, so is the hard work involved at learning about good decision making. No amount of hard, sweating work we do at the ranch, if we continue to make poor decisions and no matter how many other ranchers are doing the same thing, can bring us to that dream of successful ranching. We can be successful at cattle ranching even in spite of this modern world. But our decision making and planning has become more critical to our success than ever before.

The cow's requirements haven't changed since the beginning of time. Only our attempts at management have evolved. Nature has placed within the bovine a very fundamental system for survival. It has been our attempts at trying to change this system that has caused havoc from most of our attempts at modern cattle ranching. We have lost the very basic concept of using the free energy that originates from the sun and atmosphere and stepping back out of the way and letting the cow do what only she can do best. This wisdom cannot be purchased for any amount of money, and it will never go out of favor, yet very few take the time to stop and pick it up.

It is some of this wisdom that I have been so fortunate to have picked up here and there over the last three decades of ranching that I am going to fill these next pages. A few wise old men have shared ideas and their experiences with me. After trying all other remedies, I gave some of those ideas my best shot. What I found out was that purchasing anything in the form of inputs for the ranch was generally a failure at trying to fill my wasted attempt at good management.

I do not believe a ranch's success can be bought. It must be built and practiced like a law practice or medical practice. And what is even more alarming is that I have found that this ranching, that is successful ranching, is as much an art as it is a science.

It cannot be all taught from a book without actually experiencing it firsthand.

I have owned several different ranches and farm properties in my life with some successes and some complete failures. These pages are going to be filled with the *what-tos and what-fors* on the Rockin H Ranch property where I now live, work and play. This 1,000-acre ranch is what Gearld Fry calls a Black Jack Ridge Farm. The soils are thin. Rocks are plentiful and never in short supply. The soil cation exchange capacity, or CEC, is below 12. In the beginning we were in a drought every summer. But I don't want to get ahead of myself. Sit back and take time to read between the lines and maybe you will find something of value that I have been able to put into practice on my ranch that might save you a decade or two like some of the old wise men did for me once I got old enough to listen.

1
The Cow

IF YOU WERE TO ASK A LARGE GROUP OF CATTLEMEN at the cafe what was the most important part of a successful cattle ranch the answer would be unanimous. They would all agree that without a good set of cows you are doomed for failure. This costs many a cattleman a lifetime search for the perfect cow. Of course we know from experience that the concept of the perfect cow is as elusive as a pot of gold at the end of the rainbow. The importance of the perfect cow will be discussed in a later chapter in this book. For now we will assume that it is of most importance to obtain the perfect cow and try to understand what she would look like.

There is one attribute about the perfect cow that is far more important than any other. Without a firm foundation all structures will eventually fall. We must have a strong basis to begin with in order to have something of any value in the end. This foundation or beginning in the cow business is a live, healthy, viable calf. It would not matter the number of pretty, genetically perfect cows you have eating the perfect mix of high-brix forages with crystal clear spring water at every watering spot on the ranch. Without a live calf you are quickly doomed. And in this business that means you will have to go to work in town. There is no worse fate for a cattleman. A small, live runt of a calf is better than a dead 135-lb. pile of buzzard bait. You probably can't meet all your obligations with runt calves to sell at the end of the year, but you won't meet any of your obligations if you have nothing to take to the sale come weaning time.

The cow must calve a live calf and she must do it on her own. You can pull every calf from every cow you own for a period of time. If you have intentions of being successful you will eventually have to grow to a point to where there is not enough time in the day and night combined to pull every calf from every cow you own. Do not keep a cow on the ranch that consistently requires help at calving. It is understandable that occasionally a calf will be born breach. Even this cow should be questionable. She may be a repeat offender, and you probably won't be at her side the next time it happens. When she and her calf are looking like a million dollars take them both for a one-way ride to town. This is your best assurance she can't do it to you again.

We will be discussing the concept of risk management in many forms throughout this book. Risk management is an ongoing business practice that crosses all lines of moneymaking ventures. If we take every risk that comes our way, we will eventually fail. We must determine at an early stage of our enterprise what risks are worth taking in comparison to the possible outcome for success. If you can get your money back on a cow that has proven to be a high-risk animal, this is as good as it gets in the cattle business. Even a small loss at this time could be worth taking. It results in one risk to take the money from the sale of the cow with calving problems to pay for current expenses. To replace her we will keep back at least one quality heifer from another cow that we know as a good candidate for an easy-calving cow. It is poor risk management to keep a cow that requires help at calving even if she weans off a big calf at the end of the year.

The best place to find good-quality mother cows is deep within your own herd. There will be no other cows that can adapt to your grass, water, environment, management techniques, winter feed and all the other factors — good and bad. You can purchase cows or heifers from a good, proven herd. The success you have with these animals will not be as consistent as they were at the ranch they came from. They might have a superior set of genetics that has been proven to work under the conditions they were raised and managed. Once they have been taken out of that situation and placed into your region and management, you can expect to have a decrease in productivity and a percentage of cows that simply don't work out. You can still benefit from purchased cows, heifers and most certainly bulls, just expect a long transition period and an increase in cost per animal by at least the amount of animals that are culled in the very short run.

In the early stages of building a ranch it is important to improve the herd through purchased genetics, but don't fall for every fad and sales pitch that comes along. Your long-term goal should be to close your herd. That is develop a proven set of genetics within your own herd and then close the gate. Raise all of your replacement heifers and bulls. Gain an understanding of line breeding and use it within your herd. Retain your quality heifers from your best cows. Be extremely selective. Cull for all traits including sound udders, straight legs, broad hips, low to the ground, deep chests and barrel-shaped midsections. And certainly cull for disposition. Breed those heifers back to their sires and cull again. In the book *Animal Health and Reproduction,* Gearld Fry explained in detail how I was diluting my herd each time I would go out on the market and bring a new bull into my herd. Once I closed my herd and quit bringing in those outside bulls I began to see real genetic improvement in my cow herd. The quicker we can get our herds to the point where we are raising our own bulls and heifers, the fewer times we are forced to seek the unknown from other herds. Each time we go to the market and purchase a new bull for our herd we are diluting our chances for predictability. A closely linebred set of cows and bulls become extremely predictable in their offspring. Each new herd sire from the outside increases the possibilities of more unknown issues. The common myth that only the so-called seedstock producers breed quality bulls is designed for one thing and one thing only — to transfer wealth from your pocket to theirs. The most that these fellows promote their bulls on is how they can increase your weaning weights. As we will discuss later on in more detail, the weaning weights of your own calves is of little significance when we are working to improve net income from your ranch. And if these so-called seedstock producers were really in tune to helping the cow/calf man like they claim, they would also know that increasing weaning weights is of little help to their customers. It is predictability within the cow herd that we are seeking. And that starts with a live calf every year and at the same time every year.

Seedstock producers have a tough bill to fill as well as the commercial cowman. There are some very effective pure-breed cattlemen that have good intentions and know the business. There are also a great many that chase pounds at all costs. There should be but one main goal for the seedstock producer: to produce bulls and heifers that meet the demands of the commercial cowman. If we could take the entire lot of hobby cow people out of the commercial cow business, the playing field would be much more level. After all, the reason for feeding cattle should be to turn low-productivity land and feedstuffs into high-protein food for humans at a low cost. All cattle will wind up on a plate some day if things go as they should. The seedstock producer gets caught up in trying to produce what we tell them, and sometimes we haven't known what was in our best interest. It at first seems elementary that the more your calves weigh when it comes time to sell them the more money you will make. This could be no further from the truth for a commercial cattleman. But most of us don't know this to be true. So therefore we purchase bulls which when crossed with our cows will increase weaning weights. We keep heifers out of these crosses in order to have bigger cows that will produce bigger calves the next time. This is a vicious cycle that can trap a good cowman and put him out of business.

The EPD, *expected progeny difference,* can take the blame for some of this. But the cowman must take the bigger part of the blame. The EPD is only a tool and how we choose to work with the tool will determine what we can build. As an example, consider the EPD for milk. We know the more milk, and feed, we can put into a growing calf, the more weight he will gain. So the seedstock producers manage their cow herds to improve the EPDs on milk both in their bulls and cows. We have learned from the dairy industry a lot about milk that can be applied to beef cows. There is a direct relationship between milk production and cow maintenance. The more milk a cow produces the higher the costs will be to feed and keep that cow in good body score so she will rebreed and calve each year. Milk is an important attribute when we consider the requirements of a growing calf. What also must be put into the equation is a good balance of desired traits that work in your specific management situation. It is single-trait selection that has put our cow herds in the dire straits most are in today. High milk EPD is antagonistic to reproduction. More milk generally correlates to more reproductive problems.

The best cow in the herd will raise exactly one calf every year and never miss. She also will never eat a bite of grain, supplement, or require the use of machinery. She will never require assistance at calving and will protect her calf from predators, but will not eat you for lunch when you bring her to the corrals.

All of this — and it will never be important that she wean off the biggest calf in the herd. This will be the most profitable cow you could ever own. Notice that I never mentioned hair color, genetics or EPDs. That's because if your cows meet the description I listed in the paragraph above, the rest doesn't matter. So why do all the seedstock producers we see try to sell us on hair color, genetics and EPDs? Because we have lost sight of what makes up the best cow in our herds and because their operations are not designed with your profit in mind. Also, it is difficult for the average seedstock producer to quantify their product in terms other than weaning weights and yearly weights and so on and so forth. Most of them are also inexperienced with the term *sustainable agriculture* as we in the profitable cow/calf industry define it. If you are breeding for color, genetics, EPDs, and high weaning weights, these are the results you will achieve at your cost of profitability in your cattle operation . . . that is until you get tired of supplementing your cattle operation with other incomes and/or go broke.

At the Rockin H Ranch I want all of my cows to be defined as I mentioned above. I will not purchase or raise bulls or heifers that have been so-called "developed." These are the cattle that are supplemented with as much as 20 lbs. or more of grain daily. They are pampered, oversized, airbrushed with blow driers, and marketed as quality breeding stock. It is a shame but this describes well over 95% of all the cattle listed in the seedstock producers' catalogues. Where is the EPD for profitability? Why would I desire to wean the biggest calf in the county if it costs me more to produce him than what he will weigh out? I don't think I can ever understand why the mass majority of commercial and purebred cow/calf producers even consider buying bulls and heifers from a seedstock producer who only builds his herd as a hobby or business without any results to show his profitability on the animals he is selling us. Many times these fellows will build their entire marketing plan on how much weight their bulls will gain in a specified amount of time given abnormal rates of daily grain. We then purchase these grain-fed bulls and turn them out with our cows into a forage-based cattle operation and expect miracles. The bulls fall apart without the support of the high protein and energy derived from the daily supplement of 20 lbs. of grain. They lose weight, become lame, quit breeding cows, and soon we are forced to sell them for pennies on the dollar. There are no shortcuts. Filling the need for good genetics within your herd is a managed practice that requires a tremendous amount of time and observation. It is impossible to go to the cow store and buy what your ranch needs. You can buy the recipe and some of the ingredients. But you will have to build your herd yourself within the confines and limitations of your operation.

So how do I know which cow is the perfect cow when I'm selecting for heifer replacements for my herd? The answer is very simple. You won't know. But neither will anybody else, and that includes the seedstock producer, the university's research center, or the feed company. But what you do know that the others do not know is which cows have been performing the best within your herd on your ranch. This is paramount — which cow has calved unassisted and successfully raised her calf every single year without exception? Which cow retains a good body condition for most of the year? Which cow breeds back at the same time every year? Which cow seems more interested in foraging on her own than she does looking for a feed bucket or listening for the sound of your truck bringing a bale of hay? Which cow is no problem to bring into the corral and work? And generally speaking, which cow is your oldest? If you are culling consistently from within your herd, the oldest cows in your herd should have done all these good things and done them longer than any of the other cows. This describes the cow that produces the heifers and bulls you will keep.

We cannot keep an old cow just because we've gotten attached to her sentimental ways. As cattle ranchers we must love our children, cherish our wives, and cull the heck out of our cows. Never own a cow that you can't live without. But own a herd of cows that can make you a living. Don't follow the crowds. The latest and greatest breeds and the fancy pictures that come along with a detailed pedigree with a newly purchased cow or bull will only make good fire starter when all the hoopla is over. The only name on a registration paper that is important is the name of the person who raised her. And if you do not know every detail about how he went about that you will get more benefit from that piece of paper as a fire starter this winter than any other purpose.

You already know which cows within your herd are the most profitable. As a type, she is smaller in size. Probably about a frame score size of two to three. She probably weighs less than 1,100 lbs.; even better she may only weigh 950 lbs. Smaller cows eat less grass. It makes a lot more sense to have a herd of 950-lb. cows weaning off 450-lb. calves on grass than 1,500-lb. cows weaning off 575-lb. calves running on a creep feeder. Which calf will bring more dollars per pound? Isn't a 450-lb. calf always worth more per pound than a 600-lb. calf, no matter whether the market is high or low? Since the only thing we have to sell is pounds, shouldn't we get the most per pound that we can? The 950-lb. cow is weaning off a calf that is over 47% of her body weight. The 1,500-lb. cow is weaning off a calf of only 38% of her body weight. Many times the best cows on my ranch will wean off in excess of 60% of their own body weight with nothing added but the grass that grows on the ranch.

There is no question about what size of cow consumes the most grass in a given day. She also drinks more water, eats more salt, kills more grass with each step of her big hooves, and is a lot harder to push into the squeeze chute. It is very difficult to effectively sell the weight that is on a calf between its belly and the ground. Running big cows is kind of like checking cows with a 18-wheel over-the-road truck and trailer. The old beat up S-10 or four-wheeler is a lot more economical.

One rationale I've heard from others for keeping bigger cows over smaller cows was that when they are culled from the herd they bring so much more money at the sale barn. No doubt this is true. But with this logic I conclude that this operator is ranching in order to cash in on his cull cows. This doesn't make good economic sense. A good cow can stay on the ranch for 15 or more years. I have many cows in their twenties still having calves every year. Generally these are the 1,000-lb. cows with big bellies that winter well. Who cares if a big, oversized cull cow brings double at the sale barn as the small, efficient cow does when the big cow was culled at eight years old and giving you only six calves before her demise, and the smaller, foraging-type cow gave you seven more calves before she went to town. Smaller, efficient cows will always wean off more saleable weight through their calves than the elephants do when compared to the percentage of forage consumed and total overall efficiency. You would be better off, economically speaking, to let those old cows die peacefully on your ranch after 15 calves than to keep selling those giants after only four or five calves.

So what do you do if you go out and gather all your cows and put each one on the scale and they all weigh over 1,500 pounds? Do you immediately have an auction? Maybe you should. But first look for all the other good attributes discussed previously. Scrutinize each and every cow and determine her efficiency. Dumping every cow you own and purchasing another set of cows with other sometimes unforeseen problems is seldom the answer. You must reconcile with yourself that building a good cow herd is a *very* long-term project. It is doable if you have patience and are willing to take the time to develop an eye for what makes a good cow and don't allow your sentiments and modern trends to sway your good judgment. The same quality attributes that made up a good moneymaking cow one hundred years ago are the same today. The bovine has the unique ability to convert low-quality forages into high-value meat. She can do this with very little in terms of requirements from us. When we think we know better than she does and get in the way with other forms of inputs is when we begin falling short of maximizing every bit from our free source of sun energy possible.

I've been breeding cattle for over thirty years. It has taken the biggest part of that time to learn what I'm writing on these pages about how to ranch profitably and maintain a sustainable cow herd even during periods of low cattle prices. In my case this knowledge has come about the hard way — by trial and error. It has also come at a very high price. I could have saved myself a lot of money and grief if I had been educated in a more productive manner. We are required to look at our cow/calf operations as a business that must be profitable every year. Making ourselves alert to this nonsense of breeding cattle that do everything besides turn a profit is an absolute necessity. Breeding without profit as our foremost thought is utterly insane. Profits have absolutely no correlation with being big. I mean this in every sense of the word *big* you can come up with. It certainly does not relate to big cows and big calves. It has no connection with the size of the ranch. It certainly has no required co-existence with large farming interests or large farm machinery assets. If you are not working toward building a herd of efficient, productive cows, you would be better off selling your grass to someone else.

The cow must be a good utilizer of the forage that grows on your ranch. We cannot grow a different type of grass for each cow in the herd. We cannot purchase a set of cows from a geographical area that produces a type of grass that will not grow on our ranch and expect our cows to excel once we get them home. Nor can we spend time and effort to establish a type of grass for that set of cows that is problematic to establish and maintain. The perfect cow requires very little adjustment to fit into our system of forage management. The fewer demands we put upon her, the less stress she will experience.

We can force a cow to adjust to a lower quality of feed even after she has spent the first half of her life on a high-concentrate diet. The result will be a lower body score, lower fertility, and her efficiency will decline to a point of non-profitability. We must reach deep into our herds and select replacements that have the most attributes of the productive cows existing on the ranch. These are the cows that can produce on forage alone.

There is no place for grain feeding on a cow/calf operation. If your cows or bulls require grain feeding to remain in good body score, they are not the type of cows that will ever be able to support a ranch and its family in a commercial setting. A good commercial set of cows will excel on grass, legumes and forbs only. The rancher must become astute in selecting cattle that will not only survive on forage, but will improve from year to year. These types of cattle will appear short in stature. The cow will have a broad rear end, small round ears, a deep girth, and appear flat on the top. Some cattlemen describe as ideal a cow you could put an egg on its back and it would not roll off. Their mouths will be wide so that each bite of grass takes in a good amount of forage. The cow will produce milk high in butterfat; this can be determined by looking for shades of yellow inside the ears and within the tail switch. (It will kind of make you think of ear wax when you first see it.) We must also look for wide **escutcheon** on our cows.

The bull will look very masculine. Broad-chested, extremely large-barreled, appearing somewhat like a buffalo in stature will be your first indication that this bull can forage on his own. Both testicles should be of even size and shape, for it is the quality of the testicles on the sire that is reflected in the makeup of the udder on his daughters. The masculinity in the bull is reflected in the reproductive qualities of his offspring. In his book *Livestock Production*, Jan Bonsma describes the technique of linear measuring cattle as a tool for selecting for good reproductive traits. This is essential reading for all cow/calf ranchers. The ratio of height, length, and girth circumference is extremely important. A tall, slab-sided heifer with no girth will certainly prove to be an inefficient grazer and slow to rebreed. We must train our eyes to detect the good reproductive traits.

Disposition in the cow herd is much more than a luxury trait. A gentle cow will stay in the pasture you put her in. If mated with the similar type bull the calves will wean off with little or no objection. This type of disposition in the calves will be beneficial to the owner who chooses to feed these cattle on to finish weight. This will create less stress in the pens and will be reflected in less sickness and better weight gain. There is also a tendency for excitable cattle to produce tough, low-marbled meat. Begin selecting for good disposition in your herd from the very beginning and many management problems will be reduced.

Hair color can be a touchy subject for many ranchers. Over the years many cowmen have become partial to one color or the next. Many times this partiality has very little merit. Even in the relatively short period of time, the 35 years that I have been breeding cattle, the fad for the color of cattle has changed at least twice. At one time I could get a price premium for a spotted calf. Today a solid black animal will almost always bring a premium on the commodity markets. Quite often a rancher spends many years developing his herd in a productive manner no matter which color he started with. His selection for quality traits has proven successful. Once he has obtained a good set of proven cows, he tends to overemphasize and place more creditability to the color of his cows than the quality traits that actually helped him produce the perfect cow. This prejudice for color is very common among cattlemen.

It is a fact that the market pays premiums for black-hided cattle. I can remember a time over 30 years ago when the market paid a premium for spotted cattle, specifically crossbred Simmentals. This preference for hair color is apt to change from time to time. However, today's current trend for premiums paid for black hided cattle stems from the mass marketing of the Certified Angus Beef program originating from the late 1970s. The Angus organization has done a superb job informing the public on what a good steak looks like. Most of the non-cattle-producing population associates the name Black Angus with quality beef. Many of us in the industry know that a good steak can be hidden underneath the hide of most any color of animal. But as retailers have learned, the customer is always right. To increase the odds of getting the highest price per pound for a potload of weaned steers, one thing that can be done is to turn your cattle black. A black cow eats no more grass than a red one. And if you want to generate interest in selling either one steak, or a pen full of calves, use the name Black Angus and your responses will increase exponentially.

I do not believe in chasing fads. I was raising Simmental cattle before the explosion of the Black Angus in the United States. When Certified Angus Beef first began I did not jump on the bandwagon for over a dozen years. At a certain point I realized I was losing as much as $100 a calf simply because my cattle were spotted rather than black. Eventually I gave into the fad and turned my herd black. My cow herd is of higher quality now than it was thirty-some-odd years ago. This is due mostly to the improvement of my selection for reproductive traits and very little if any to do with the change in color of the hide over the beef. We must be tuned into reality that ranching is the production of a quality food for the public. We must not close our eyes to the fact that however isolated we may appear on our ranch that the ultimate consumer has a great deal to say about our product. We may be able to produce the perfect cow, but if no one will buy it at a fair market price we will be out of business very quickly.

As the market for Black Angus cattle has grown so rapidly, so has the number of seedstock producers of black cattle. What has not kept up with the pace is the number of these producers who are producing quality bulls and heifers. There are more places to purchase Angus bulls than any other breed. It seems that many pure-breed cattlemen have found a market for anything black hided. This in turn has made it very difficult to locate quality, reproductive Black Angus bulls and heifers. Many uniformed ranchers have been purchasing their bulls from these seedstock producers who are first concerned with color and secondly concerned with weight gains, neither of which have any importance to the reproductive qualities of the cow herd. A black bull of low reproductive quality can be made to look quite impressive to the public by feeding him 25 lbs. of grain and alfalfa hay per day and grooming him like a prize poodle. The less informed cattleman comes along and purchases what looks like a robust forage machine. Once the grain-filled monster is dumped out in the pasture with his herd, the problems begin. He is no longer getting the high concentrate grain. He is expected to forage — walking and eating, a system that he knows very little about. And even worse, the high-grain diet has permanently reduced his good semen count below an acceptable level. Even if he does breed a few cows before his feet go bad, his offspring will replicate his inefficiencies as a forager. The production and selling of such bulls simply because they are black has been the main culprit in perpetuating poor-quality reproductive traits among the Black Angus breed. This is just another example of how single-trait selection damages the quality of the cow herd.

A cow that sheds her thick hair coat early in the spring will tend to be more productive than one that does not. The farther south we go, the less hair we want on our cattle. A Nebraska ranch can keep cows with a much thicker hair coat than a ranch in Alabama. This is one of the reasons why it is best to produce our own replacement bulls and heifers than go to the market. A productive cow in Nebraska might never be able to adapt to the heat in Alabama.

Unlike stock on the New York Stock Exchange, our stock out on the ranch is not near as portable. Some cattlemen never understand this point. They want to buy, sell and trade cattle like stocks and bonds. A bond may pay the same return in spite of its owner's attempt of management and storage of the document. The return paid on cattle is directly related to the management and storage of the herd. This return can be comparable to paper stocks, but very few times can a herd of cattle be cashed in on. The perfect cow is only perfect because of the management of selection, matching of forages and climates, and the willingness to spend what in most cases is a lifetime commitment to planned growth and improvement.

2
Grass Management

THE CATCH PHRASE OF MY GENERATION at the university, Natural Resources Conservation Service (NRCS), Extension offices and other so-called professional agricultural libraries has got to be MIG, *management intensive grazing*. What I object to most concerning this whole MIG thing is the light-heartedness and careless misuse of the term and its practice. For this type of practice to be proficient, it must be included in an entire method of a well-planned ranch business program. This entire method must take the entire ranch into consideration as a whole. Allan Savory calls this approach holistic in his book *Holistic Management*.

A ranch, depending upon its size, might have many divisions, profit centers, segments, enterprises, etc., but none can be completely isolated from the rest. As a whole unit the ranch exists and profits from the symbiotic relationship of the parts and pieces that make up the ranch. Any change that is made on the ranch in one area will have an effect on many other areas. It's like having a bunch of rowdy kids in a small rowboat. Any movement by any one child will have an impact on the balance of the boat in the water. What must be accepted early on is that if we have too much movement by too many different kids at the same time the boat may well capsize and everyone gets dumped.

In ranching, or any other profit-motivated organization, this sometimes ends in bankruptcy. All changes on the ranch affect other parts of the ranch and have tremendous consequences on the whole. If one makes the decision to mechanically harvest forage from a paddock this summer there is a direct change that will occur on all the other paddocks on the ranch and the soil structure will begin a change because of that decision. The effect on the microbiology in the soil will be significant on the hay paddock for many reasons. This paddock would have been taken out of the rotation for a significant amount of time allowing the roots to increase in size over the root size of the plants in all the other paddocks. This will have not only an effect on water infiltration in the hay paddock, but because we will have placed more grazing pressure on all the other paddocks in the rotation, we will have altered the distribution of fertility (manure), changed growth patterns, redirected solar energy concentration, effected mineral development, and many other changes that take place on the ranch because of the tremendous results from a different area of herd impact. We will have compacted certain soil areas on the ranch due to heavy equipment usage, our decrease of cattle drinking water will have resulted in some areas and increased in others changing the growth of at least some forage around certain watering sights that may or may not have accepted the additional pressure at that time of year, and the list is infinite.

The holistic approach is a critical concept of management that must be increasingly emphasized to avoid a snowball effect of bad decisions. There is much more to intensive-type grazing than simply subdividing pastures into small, five-acre paddocks.

It has been proven in grazing tests that by limiting the time cattle are allowed to graze in a pasture and then allowing the pasture a period of time to rest can increase grass production. However, for MIG to be successful many attributes must be included in the practice as a whole. Throwing up a few electric fences and moving cattle from pasture to pasture every two to seven days without taking into consideration the nutrient levels of the soil will increase the carrying capacity only marginally. The entire program must be reviewed if we expect results that can make a significant increase in carrying capacity.

A distinction must be made early on in this managed grazing system between carrying capacity and stock density. The total number of mature cattle — which is roughly speaking about the number of 1,000 lb. cows, that can be grazed over a period of one year on a particular farm or ranch — is the carrying capacity. In contrast, stock density is the number of mature cattle that are grazing in a particular pasture during a given day or part of a day. Quite often we refer to stock density in terms of number of cows per acre or pounds of cattle per acre. A stock density of 200,000 lbs. per acre, or 200 cows on a one-acre pasture for one day is very common on a well-managed grazing program. The possibility of having a 200 cow per acre carrying capacity ranch for the year is absurd.

In continuous grazing systems in my part of southern Missouri, most ranches boast a six- to 10-acre-per-cow carrying capacity with additional hay feeding for three to five months. This would compare to some of the ranches out west in the brittle environments where ranch carrying capacities would range from 25- to over 100-acres-per-cow carrying capacity. It must be recognized from the onset that one of the best ways to increase carrying capacity of a ranch is to increase stock density. If we are able to increase the stock density of most or all of our individual pastures, our total grass production will increase both in quality and in quantity and our feeding of mechanically harvested feeds will decrease significantly in a very short amount of time. Not only will our cost of winter feedstuffs decrease both in labor and in number of bales of hay fed, but the total number of cows, or carrying capacity, on the ranch will increase. This increase in the production of grass, legumes and forbs is the foundation of all things that matter concerning MIG.

I was visiting a farmer on the western side of our county last month who grows out Holstein heifers on his 140 acres. He is a proponent of MIG and is proud of his accomplishments, one of which he's quick to point out is his ability to grow out over 200 heifers at a time on his 140-acre farm. On the surface this sounds like tremendous carry capacity even for a lush Missouri set of grass in early spring. After discussing his program more in depth, he slowly reveals his outside inputs. To keep his heifers growing he supplements them with about 5 lbs. a day of 15% protein in the form of a grain ration. He also keeps a mineral feeder full of free-choice minerals year-round. In addition, he maintains a stack of alfalfa hay outside, only because he doesn't have a barn big enough to store it inside. I could not get a reliable figure on the amount of hay he is feeding daily, but I would venture to say by looking at the size of his hay stack that it would be a considerable amount.

It is only natural for an operator to desire his program to be successful. Sometimes his desire can be so strong that good judgment is left in the seat of the pickup truck. It is very obvious to me that there are many proponents of MIG that are like this Holstein guy. They are not fully aware of the amount of outside inputs they are contributing in order to get their grazing system to fit specific pegs and holes they have designed.

The other extreme I see with MIG is the operator who is unaware or who will not acknowledge the fact that while he is not only subdividing his pastures and maintaining a better crop of forage residue, he also is doing a better job of maintaining his soil nutrients. If many of these new proponents of MIG would have been improving the condition of their soils before MIG as they are afterwards, they may have never gone to the effort of all the electric fences and tiny paddocks on their farms and ranches. Most of these grazers will up their fertilizer programs substantially and improve their stands of grasses and legumes once they start analyzing their systems closer. This increase in soil fertility and total grass management is what makes the greatest change in forage quantity and quality.

What may be unknown to most of these operators is that real improvements to soil fertility come more through herd impact and rest than through the standard NPK regiment. Rotational grazing incorporated with a total management system will only complement those forages grown. It is this total management system, or what some have entitled the holistic approach, that makes the biggest difference on soil fertility and ultimately net profits from the grazing animal. We now add in the inexact science of manipulating elements in the soil by making orthodox attempts at plant feeding. This non-sustainable attempt at promoting the growth of forages can empty the bank account while also falling short of anything close to year-round grazing.

It is rest following high stock densities in each paddock that can increase soil nutrient levels, water infiltration, mineral recycling, and ultimately increased solar collection through more plants per unit of land. Harsh effects from droughts are minimized as in many cases the holistic-managed ranch proves impervious to the local drought while its neighbors are forced to resort to feeding hay and or selling cattle.

Through a planned grazing program we are making an attempt at scheduling rest periods of two, three or more months for each paddock. It should become apparent to readers that to rest all paddocks for a minimum of three months, or 90 days, we must have at least a total of ninety-one paddocks to accomplish this rotation. This style of planned grazing is far more involved than the five-paddock rotation alluded to in simple MIG systems or rotational grazing.

Of course, one must never forget the fundamental goal of grass production ultimately aimed to produce pounds of beef at a profit. This amount of profit is in the end calculated at an amount of dollars profit per acre. The reason being for this is that land itself is generally limited and is the most expensive input. If all ranchers had equal access to an unlimited amount of free grazing land (provided no governmental intervention), we would have little to no interest in stocking rates and carrying capacities.

We know from our own experiences when total cow numbers are low our other costs of inputs such as winter feed, fall accordingly. If I had a 300-acre field of grass here in southern Missouri and only six cows and a bull to graze, I would have nothing to gain from intensive management of that field. All I would need to do is gather and sell the calves each year and the overabundance of forage and nature herself would do the rest or so it would seem. Due to our climate and humidity, however, our pastures would first revert to brush due to undergrazing and poor forage management. Eventually the brush would be overtaken by larger woody species and a forest would emerge.

It is mostly, if not solely, important to manage that field for higher production because of its high cost. Few families could make a living selling the calves from only six cows. I want to emphasize the importance of this concept of stocking rate being terrifically important to profits, particularly when the young rancher is carrying a high debt load on that property. A young rancher might be required to carry more cows on his ranch than he will once he becomes older and no longer has a debt to service with earnings from his calf crop each year. Fewer cows can always be run easier and more economically on the same ranch than a larger herd can. However, with the cost of the grazing land being the largest input cost, particularly in the early growth stages of a cow herd, it is absolutely imperative that efficiency of pounds of beef produced per acre at the lowest cost be foremost in our thoughts.

This expense of land is categorized as an overhead cost. Stan Parsons has brought to our attention that there are only three ways to improve profits on the ranch. Number one is to increase gross margins. Second is to increase turnover. Third is to lower overhead costs. Since this cost of land is considered somewhat of a fixed cost, the interest or rent remains the same no matter how many cows we graze during the year. But the more cows we can successfully carry during the year the lower our individual overhead cost per cow will be. In most regards we can graze six cows just as easily as we can graze sixty cows. The main difference? It will take an extra thirty seconds per day to rotate the herd on the latter.

Here in southern Missouri I see room for grass improvement on almost every pasture I see as I drive down the road. As I travel across various parts of the United States my eyes are always looking through the viewfinder of grass. My obsession with grass would drive the non-agricultural-minded person insane. Looking at pastures out West, I marvel at how well cattle do on what seems such a small amount of available pasture. The prairie ground of the Flint Hills of Kansas produces some of the richest grasslands of our nation. This is done naturally without the addition of fertilizer. In fact, some prairie grass would die if we were to add a single load of nitrogen. Native grasses have provided an inexpensive forage base for cattle for generations. As our population increases and land is consumed by hobby farmers and subdivisions, only land that is considered less desirable for human habitat will be left for pastureland. The land that is left will have to be more productive than ever. Rotational grazing combined with true grass management will and has become more important than ever before.

Almost all of my experience with grass management has been in these southern Missouri hills and "hollers." I cannot discuss how the rancher in Colorado might increase his carrying capacity because I have never ranched in Colorado. But I have spent my lifetime working at grazing cattle in Missouri and can give insight on how to increase cow numbers on a given acreage in this state. I do believe that many of my techniques could be partially modified to suit other areas. Even though soils are quite different between Missouri and Colorado, the concepts of improving grass through the practice of land management can be taken west, or any other direction as far as that goes.

Some would say it is overgrazing through overstocking with cattle that diminishes pastures the most. In many cases, when management makes planning a priority on the ranch the stocking rates are increased. So maybe we were not *over*stocked to begin with, just *under*planned. The actual cause of forage shortages most often can be attributed to being *under*-rested. It is not having too many cows per acre-stock density — that causes us to run short of forage. We can run 500,000 lbs. to the acre; some ranches have run as much as 1,000,000 lbs. of cows to the acre. This is equivalent to 1,000 cows averaging 1,000 lbs. each. It is the period of rest following this heavy herd impact that is essential. We must not allow the herd to return to this grazed paddock before plants have ample time not only to grow back above ground, replacing what was eaten, but to grow a new, strong root system as well.

We can, with planning, seldom, if ever, run out of grass. Foremost in our thoughts each day as we work the ranch is the recycling of available minerals and the best utilization of our energy source, the sun. We can choose to mine our resources like a coal pit, using it up until there is nothing left. Or we can put into action a system that we can use to determine our stocking rates and carrying capacity instead of using what forage is standing until it is gone and is evident that we are overstocked.

The predominate grass in southern Missouri is tall fescue. Fescue is one of the most forgiving grasses I have ever used. A herd of cattle can eat fescue down to the ground during the winter months, and given a proper amount of time for recovery and soil nutrients and moisture, it will revive and flourish. If the same ground is allowed to be eaten down by overgrazing for long periods of time the grass will disappear and rocks will replace the stand of grass, just as if they were spread on top of the ground by a dump truck.

So what is the carrying capacity of a Missouri ranch? The real estate salesman will tell potential buyers one cow per four acres. The out-of-state buyer will tell you one cow per 10 acres after three years of mismanagement. I have pastured 350 weaned calves on 40 acres of mixed grasses from July through December. I have wintered 300 cows on 400 acres of stockpiled fescue from October through April with scarcely any feeding of hay, except when the grass was covered with a thick layer of ice and the cattle had difficulty breaking through. I believe the same pastures could have handled another 100 head. On another set of pastures that I purchased for a cow/calf herd the results were not quite so impressive. When the ranch was first purchased the grass had been allowed to decline to minimal standards. Seed, lime and fertilizers had not been applied, nor any form of planned grazing for about 20 years. The 1,000 acres of pasture was only feeding about 120 cow/calf pairs and a lot of hay was being fed.

I had known the ranch and its prior owner for many years. The ranch had capacity to produce a lot more than it had been allowed for the last 20 years. This ranch is equipped with one of the most perfect natural land structures for cattle raising that I have ever seen on a single piece of property. Twenty percent of the land was in river bottom; 70% in ridgeland grasses. The balance was in timber well suited for protecting cattle from bad weather. The rich bottom ground was best suited for fast-growing annuals. After a change in management the ranch has summer Sudan grass where 500 cow/calf pairs can cell graze on five acres at a time and within a few good rains return back to the first cell and begin the rotation again. This is alternated in the early fall with annual rye grass no-tilled, with minimums spent for fuel and labor to grow a winter feed, a feed that requires only pasture management. The high ridge grassland is fescue stockpiled for winter grazing.

The ranch has a thin layer of soil, but this is not entirely a negative. There is just enough rock and solid ground to keep the cattle out of the mud, even during the worst of the winter. A winding creek entering the south-center of the ranch and exiting on the north at almost dead center with the east and west fencelines provides an excellent source of water for livestock. Fresh springwater flowing from a dozen or more natural springs — requiring no source of power and certainly no problems when powerlines fail — provides year-round fresh water. The ranch possesses all of these natural attributes, yet previous owners did not see or did not take the time to develop the potential this great ranch holds for grass production.

These annuals are only a quick fix for improving carrying capacity. The long-term goal is to improve the pasture sward with additional legumes, the primary feedstuff being white clover. A 40% to 60% stand of white clover with a mixture of red clover, alfalfa, alsike, chicory, plantain, vetch, orchard grass, Kentucky bluegrass, crab grass, lamb's-quarter, pigweed, ragweed, dandelion and other forbs and herbs. Managing a ranch almost totally from a perennial mindset is where the efficiency increases exponentially. Even an annual like lespedeza can be managed where grazing time is minimized late in the season to allow some of the plants to make seed for the seasons to follow. I frequently have found that purchasing seed for new forages can be an unnecessary expense. With high-stock-density grazing the soil becomes disturbed with animal impact from hoof action to the point that seeds that have lain dormant for generations become mobilized and germinate.

Not only has man tried his best at forage improvement on this ranch through planting of seeds, but also the pollinators, livestock carrying seed from here to there, and even the wind plays a role of moving seeds from one point to another. The conditions at the time determine which seeds germinate and their success to a point. Over time it is a form of adaptation that fills the sward with grasses, legumes, forbs, and herbs that are best suited for this ranch. A thick sward of grasses of many varieties and species, maybe 20 to 30 or more, will appear as the soil improves, whether I plant seed or not.

I have read that the grass swards of Kentucky at the turn of the 18th century perhaps had as many as 80 different varieties of forages. With this multi-species forage smorgasbord the livestock can better select for health than I can with a mineral bag. And the cost of their choice to me will be only the opening and closing of a gate. My region is blessed with a diversity of land types. This diversity is what makes our grassland superior to many. This ranch is the best example I have seen to illustrate this phenomenon. The hills and hollers of Missouri create small, fertility-rich acres of bottom ground that hold water quite well during dry periods. The tops of the hillsides, even with thin layers of fertile soils, can produce large quantities of mixed forages. These rocky hills also give a rancher an area to graze cattle in during the wet and soggy months. The bottom pastures can be rested during the wet periods and the hard-surfaced hillsides will keep the cattle out of the mud, yet allow for pasturing all winter long. It is along these keylines that new fences are constructed to separate one soil type from another on the same farm.

What is even more amazing is what happens between the rocky hills and the rich, fertile bottom ground. All ranchers will agree that water is the most vital resource for cattle. These hollers that are left between the hills and bottom ground will quite often contain natural springs that flow year-round. The water is freeze-proof in the winter, requiring no manufactured power whatsoever to produce and maintain. The spring water is so pure and clean I will drink it myself, even during the hot summer months when the trickling spring water remains chilled. It is these springs that I have found to be so impressive on this ranch. There is a spring in almost every holler that exists on this ranch. Sometimes there are two and three springs up the same holler. All these springs run into one of two mid-sized creeks that run from one end of the ranch to the other.

About 20% of the pastures are fertile bottoms with the remaining being on the rocky hillsides. Even though I speak of these bottoms as fertile, they were a far cry from optimum when I first purchased this ranch. I dumped 300 head of cows on the ranch in July, expecting them to begin calving in September. I was feeding hay by mid-November. The potential was there, but not yet developed. Dry, hot weather during the summer dried the springs and the shallow soils, with poor water infiltration due mainly to lack of management, also dried up most of the poor quality forages. The previous owner did no managed grazing. Cattle were for the most part continuous grazed. Very few if any of the deep-rooted herbs like chicory or plantain or the nitrogen-translocating legumes were available to work their wonders. The cattle roamed the ranch choosing their favorite tastes, leaving the more undesirable plants to remain until last. Gradually the ranch reached a point where mostly the undesirable plants dominated and the few cattle that the ranch could support on poor-quality forages were taking the ranch to even lower levels of production, with the cattle trails evident from one watering hole to the next.

As soon as I purchased the ranch I began taking soil tests. I analyzed each and every pasture for its content of grass types. Even though I saw the tremendous potential this ranch had it would be several years before it could be self-sustaining. The 120 pairs that were being run before was an understocked rate for a ranch this size in Missouri with good management. The 300 head I placed on the ranch consumed the available grass in less than a few short months. Still, for the land mass this was not a lot of cattle during years with average precipitation for a southern Missouri ranch that is managed correctly.

I knew the least expensive fertilizer comes from the rear end of a cow, and by stocking this ranch with as many cattle as is practical and rotating between pastures frequently, I could improve the available grass. I had no expectation of profits any time soon. The idea was to get the soil to a higher level as soon as possible in the most economic way possible. With a limited budget the possibility of bringing all pastures up to soil test with purchased chemical fertility at one time was not an option. That is seldom a practical solution anyway. There will always be a certain amount of what you put on top of these hills, as far as adding soil amendments goes, that will wind up flowing down the hollers during a hard rain and ending up in the creeks and washing off the ranch altogether. Not only is this not economical, it is not environmentally safe at high levels. Therefore, it is feasible to make changes to the soil in a systematic plan over a period of time. During this time the ranch is not expected to be profitable or self-sustaining. Not only is the washing away of soil nutrients a detriment, there is the possibility of drought. If we apply high levels of, say, nitrogen on all pastures in the beginning, and the rain does not fall as expected, not only does the grass not grow but it can be killed or set way back.

So the process began. Field by field the fertilizer, lime and overseeding commenced. Our soils, even though diverse, require some of the same nutrients to produce grass whether in the bottoms or on the hills. A split application of soil nutrients is best as a single application in the early spring without nitrogen, with another application in the fall with the required nitrogen added. A continuation of broadcasting seed with the fertilizer is by far the most economical method. This can be done anytime you fertilize, however, never miss the opportunity to broadcast seed with the spring application. I prefer to fertilize along with added legume seed from mid-February through the end of March. The thawing and freezing of the ground during this time period will facilitate adequate seed coverage.

Apply nitrogen with the rest of the fertilizer late in August or early September. This will push the fall growth forward and allow for stockpiled grasses for winter feed rather than baled hay. I will address on winter feeds more in the next few chapters. The spreading of lime is without a doubt the most important of all tools, except water, for improving soil fertility. There is a lag of time between when lime is applied and when fertilizer should be spread. I recommend that lime be applied one year before fertilizer is applied. This allows time for the slow activation that lime requires to begin its work. Application of lime can change the pH of the soil. Application of other soil nutrients can alter the pH as well. To get the optimum from applied fertilizer, the pH must be adequate. The Natural Resources Conservation Service (NRCS) states that it takes a year for lime to move down through one inch of soil. Of course, if the soil sample comes back with no requirement for lime does this mean you can proceed with the other soil nutrients? My experience has been that I can only use soil tests as a guide to increasing soil fertility. On ground that has been abused, as these 1,000 acres have been, I find that the hillsides will actually be deficit of about three ton of lime per acre. The bottom ground will need about 1.5 tons per acre to begin with; taking into account at all times the nutrient balancing in the soil. We must be aware of how the application of limestone has been historically used to change an acidic soil to a more alkaline state, raising the pH level.

Increasing the level of calcium through this limestone application can be beneficial, but soil requirements must be met and exceeding these requirements with soil amendments not only devastates the bank account, but might tie up necessary soil elements needed for healthy forage production. We must never forget that at the same time we change the pH in the soil with limestone, applications of other such fertility ingredients like phosphorus also alters soil pH. If we choose to apply soil fertility improvements in this manner, we must use experts in the field of soil nutrition and become somewhat of an expert ourselves in fertility management. We must develop an understanding of cation exchange capacity (CEC), the level at which the clay particles in the soil have the ability to exchange nutrients. The balance between calcium and magnesium becomes extremely critical, as well as most all the other elements beyond simple NPK.

The soil analysis results will display the organic matter level for each sample. As not being an element sold at most fertilizer plants, it will for the most part be ignored. In fact, if we are to make economical improvements in our soil's production capacity it is the change in organic matter that will matter the most. By increasing organic matter we will feed our humus level wherein lie the nutrients that become available to the plants now growing and about to begin growing on the ranch.

The element carbon, being of most importance, is another not available for sale in a bag or bulk at the fertilizer plant. But without the addition of carbon to our soils, improvements to fertility are mostly in vain. I made what additions to the soil I felt

I could afford in the way of recommended soil amendments from the university soil analysis. Some areas of the ranch received these purchased products, but most did not. I simply did not have the cash. My past experiences began to haunt me in the fact that over the last 20-some-odd years I couldn't say for sure if all the so-called experts on soil and their suggested treatments ever really paid back with profits from the sale of beef.

I had hungry cattle and a poor supply of forage to work with and even less capital to expend. A search like no other began for a solution or solutions that could help get this poor ranch into a profitable situation. I began reading everything I could find on growing forages and soil amendments. To apply all of the recommended nutrients on every acre at once was simply not affordable. And I wasn't sold on the idea of chemical fertilizers anyway. I had never seen any substantial improvements from these costly amendments in the past.

Among many of the books I read there seemed to be a steady line about the organic matter level in our soils. This is the line item that always showed up on the soil analysis, but was never given any credit by the people that were supposed to be helping me manage my ranch. In cowboy terms, I slowly gathered that it is this organic matter that in a roundabout way improves the level of humus in the soil. With substantial humus we can gain the ability to hold and even sequester the needed nutrients that one needs to grow more plants. I also found among these words the ability that carbon bestowed upon our chances for increasing the organic matter in our soils. This line of thinking flies in the face of the so-called experts I had run across up to this point in my ranching career of over 20 years. How could it be that the things I needed most were those I could not purchase from a fertilizer dealer and were routinely ignored by the university crowd? And then, like a boulder falling from the sky, I saw the difference. I had been taught that to increase productivity I had to feed my plants in the same approach as dumping a bag of grain into a feed trough until it is gone and then returning to the merchant with more cash to buy more feed, over and over again, this being a cycle that helps everyone else in the economic feed trough to a great extent, yet my cattle are still screaming for something more.

What I had not discovered up until this point is that my attempt at feeding a plant had been in vain and was a complete losing battle before I even started. I am not the one whose responsibility it is to feed the plant. It is the responsibility of the soil to feed the plant. To allow the soil to feed my plants I must get out of the highly complex soil matrix and let the microbiology of the soil begin to work its miracle. The advent of NPK analysis — giving us incomplete and inaccurate diagnosis and treatment for sickened soils — results in a chance for increased fertility at a sustainable level to next to zero.

This new method (or is it the oldest of all methods?) of building up the soil from organic matter, at least new to me, began to make a great deal of sense. I began to implement what I was discovering on my own, mostly through reading the accounts of others who had success with this system. Many times over the years, concerning other areas of management besides forage, I had repeated the old adage that it's always best to use what you've got before looking elsewhere for something better. And for the most part as ranchers we already have what we need on the ranch to improve forage growth. We must learn how to utilize this organic matter and all that it entails to make profits on the ranch.

All the time I was improving the soil nutrients artificially, I also rotated the cattle regularly from pasture to pasture to get a better distribution of natural fertilizer. It was also important that I fed the hay in a different location each day. Unrolling the round bales of hay instead of feeding in the same place every day better spreads the cow manure, urine and grass seeds that are in the fed hay. One requirement was that I had to have a better way to control the location of the cattle. I needed to group these cattle into one single bunch on small areas for short periods of time to control manure distribution and herd impact. No longer could the cattle be allowed to continuous graze across the entire ranch. Without constant herding, my only alternative was a massive fencing project.

With this being my only practical chance for improving the forage, I started fencing with high-tensile, single-wire electric fence from one end of the ranch to the other creating a system of paddocks and grazing cells that would eventually advance to over 100 different grazing pastures. This practice provided the best results even without the cost of additional inputs, other than fencing, or extensive soil analyses.

I have grave doubts whether or not the initial cost of purchased soil nutrients improved my chances substantially for better stands of grass and productivity. I could see no difference in the few paddocks that I had chemically fertilized, and I had no money to spend on the others anyway. Our long-range plan must be devised to reduce our dependency upon purchased inputs, but not a complete separation from adding the needed ingredients for success. If the soil is deficit of calcium and magnesium and other requirements of good soil, we must continue with these purchased inputs for the soil if we desire rapid change. Some of these and other minerals can be fed directly to cattle, but this type of management has no basis for long-term sustainability. We can hand feed cattle daily at great cost of inputs and labor. Or we can devise a plan to feed the soil when it is more convenient to do so and allow nature to supply additional resources. The latter will prove to be more cost-effective as well as more palatable to all who breathe the same air on the ranch.

The long-range grass management plan will include a generous amount of growing legumes on most every acre of grass-producing soil on the ranch. Legumes are laborers who require very little pay. Deep-rooted herbs like chicory and plantain, and even the forage alfalfas reach deep to the depths of our soils to bring forth minerals and other needed nutrients that have been farmed out of the top layers of our fields. White clovers, being the easiest to establish, should be a cornerstone of all legume mixes. This legume only grows to a low height, but can cover the bare, open soil areas where once only rocks and brush occupied valuable land. Lespedeza broadcasted at the time in winter when the soil is freezing and thawing daily by cold, damp nights and warming sun will appear in clusters when the heat of August burns all other green grasses down to non-production. Red clover broadcast along with the fertilizer at the rate of only ¼ lb. per acre on an irregular basis will provide a legume that cattle will clean the pasture of when first entering a new grazing cell early in the growing season. Once my soil was brought to sobriety again and left the drugged effect of chemical fertilizers behind, forages began to sprout that I had never planted. Good-quality grasses, legumes, herbs and all sorts of green plant life will come to life on our ranches from seeds that come by way of previous soil managers and pollinators. Soils distributed by hoof action will germinate seeds into plants that have not been seen growing for decades. The seeds are already in the soil, lying dormant, waiting for the manager to put them to use. The deep-reaching roots of the grazing-type alfalfa and chicory will bring up nutrients not available to shallow-rooted plants. These and other legumes will extract the required nitrogen from the air. This fact, not a minor decrease in purchased soil nutrients, will reduce input costs while at the same time improve efficiency by increasing carrying capacity. Calves suckling cows will gain weight all year long, supplementing themselves along the way on these legumes that yield at varying times through the growing season. Nursing cows will experience improved conception rates through better nutrition received from these high-protein, mineralized feeds. Hair coats will become slick and shining. Eye problems, feet abnormalities, and parasite infestations are just a few of the common disorders associated with raising cattle that will diminish — all because of better management of our soils through the simple practice of soil biological improvements. All of these legumes, grasses, herbs and forbs working with nature will help bring black ink to a ranch, not in contrast or opposition to soil re-building, but as unpaid employees who never tire.

The process is slow as nature operates on its own schedule. And, because of the unpredictable characteristics of the soil, water and air, time is our comrade. When after a single application of legume seed a drought comes upon us, the seed might not germinate immediately. Or other nutrients in the soil needed for a quick start on growth may be lacking. At first our thoughts will be that any failure is due to the plan. In fact, this type of result will no doubt appear many times in our process of improving our grasses and soils toward better productivity. We must not allow a single failure, or even multiple short-term failures to deter us from our long-range plan to improve our nutrient level and ultimately our stand of grasses in all pastures. A season of short rainfall will not destroy the legume seed. It is still in the ground waiting for the proper alignment of conditions to sprout its head above the soil and begin working on behalf of the space it now occupies on your ranch. One season might provide an abundance of white clover. The following year red clover may cover the pasture like a sea of purple heads bobbing in the wind. The pasture that contains a salad mixture of legumes and grasses will provide a better supply of cattle feed from year to year. One year's conditions may provide a situation more suitable for cool-season grasses longer in the season. And then, with hardly any required notice, the summer heat may at once take hold. If the conditions are favorable, the lespedeza will produce and carry the load of working for the space it occupies beneath the soil. And when its season is right, each plant will spread its roots deep beneath the soil. The alfalfa plant's roots can extend its fingerlike probes some 30 feet through all soils, rocks, hardpan and crevices searching out moisture and minerals and other benefits for healthy legumes and grasses. The legume roots will locate soil-building materials which are either not available or not in sufficient quantities on the surface.

While the legume is improving its house of soil-building materials the ever-important earthworm will appear in the quality soils first. He will make his contribution to soil building while also traveling beneath the soil's surface. His castings are rich food for soil and his actions beneath the legumes will loosen the soil for rainwater to more easily penetrate the once-hard-packed topsoil. Now we have workers on the job, each doing what nature has designed. Long-fingered roots of legumes bring forth soil-building nutrients from deep below the soil surface. Earthworms that seem to appear from nowhere have been deposited by Mother Earth to join in construction of better soils, all working separately but as organized tradesman on a construction site to complete the project according to the master blueprint.

The proverbial snowball is now rolling. Our management of the cattle becomes even more important. We continue to graze each pasture not for months at a time without rest, but in cells. We move the cattle from grazing cell to grazing cell by simply opening one gate and then closing the gate behind the last slow-moving grandma cow that takes her time. She has no worry about available forage that the young aggressive heifers run for when they hear the rattle of the chain that opens the gate for fresh-tasting, rich legume pasture.

Even the cows and calves that deposit their urine and manure are contributing to the project of soil building. Unlike before, when continuous grazing allowed the cattle to walk over large sections of the ranch creating long, deep trails of grassless gullies, they are now content wandering with their heads down in lush clovers. Then within just a few days while the grasses are still above ankle high, another gate is opened to fresher pasture once again. When the chain on the gate rattles, heads pop up and the excitement of fresh grass and legumes motivates all the cattle to migrate through yet another open gate. The process continues. Workers beneath the soil perform tasks no creation of man can approximate. Our management of the cattle on the surface actually creates more grass than if we had no cattle at all. This same ranch that only five short years ago barely kept 120 head of cows and calves fed is now grazing over 500 pair with capacity increasing as management improves below and above the surface of the soil.

It is not only the riches of the castings left by the worms and the nutrients brought up from the deep-rooted legumes that improve the stands of grasses. Both create crevices beneath the surface that act as rainwater canals to collect what moisture nature provides. Thousands and thousands of gallons of rainwater that once hit the hard surface of the soil left the ranch by traveling the way of the watershed following the path of our creeks, in the Missouri river, resting ultimately in the Gulf. This water is now able to penetrate through the legumes and grasses and find paths through our miniature constructed canals. The rainwater that once left the ranch as quickly as it arrived is now held and put to work toward soil restoration and soil building. The moisture-holding capacity of the soil is increased tenfold or more.

This soil building project means the many phases and steps are all working for the same end goal. We fed the soil so it could feed the cattle. A bag of legume seed ultimately turns into the equivalent tractor-trailer loads of feed, if we were to measure our production by harvesting our grasses mechanically instead of allowing the cattle to do that job as their part of this master plan. Our unpaid workers beneath the top level of soil are building humus without the high cost of purchased nitrogen. In the beginning stages I made costly purchases of nitrogen in the fall to achieve forage growth. But now I realize some of the pastures that never received any of that costly input are improving at a rate as fast as the pastures that did receive nitrogen. It is the daily rotation of the herd moving from paddock to paddock that is bringing the greatest change in soil nutrition. This change is all for the good. And the only cost is opening and closing a gate each day. When a large group of cattle is moved into a new pasture some of the litter is stomped into the ground. This adds needed carbon to the soil structure. The ultimate grazing plan allows only one bite of each blade of grass. The more grass we have above the soil level, the more root development below. Without adequate roots plants cannot contribute to soil restoration.

The increase in soil nutrition provides a better balance of nutrient-dense forages. Moving the cattle frequently into higher quality forage from pasture to pasture significantly reduces parasite infestation. No longer is it necessary to purchase expensive wormers, delicers, and other parasite control products to pour down the cattle's backs. By eliminating this unnecessary practice, taught to us by large corporations manufacturing and marketing these costly inputs, we have allowed the natural ability the cow possesses to operate. Her resistance to parasites is no longer encumbered by these poured-on modern materials. Now she herself has rid her body of the high levels of parasites that once lowered her metabolism. Our interference with her plan by applying chemicals to her back only increased production costs and ensured a continued supply of these parasites. And now that we are no longer poisoning the cow we have solved our summer fly problems as well.

After enough time has passed, the chemical residue has declined in the urine and cow pies which once lingered in the pastures for months eventually disappearing. Dung beetles have returned to help us in our long-range plan of soil fertility management. Not only do these unpaid workers transport the cow piles to a level in the organic mass where needed nutrients are utilized, but something almost magical begins. This cycle has now evolved to a critical level, the critical level required for systems approach management. It is a system that nature has provided once we remove our uneducated practice of interference. The chemicals we once poured on the backs of our cows to eliminate worms and lice provided residue in the cow piles that killed our population of dung beetles. Now the dung beetles have returned to work for us. The removal of the cow piles by way of the dung beetles within just a few hours, also has taken with it the fly in its pupae stage. Now the fly problem on the cow has been reduced to a level of near extinction. Flies that once required cow piles as a haven for reproduction have vanished.

Every few days we open another gate to yet another fresh pasture of grass, legumes, and natural forbs and herbs, a pasture not littered with a single cow pile, pasture where our unpaid workers at and below soil level have been laboring for our benefit, for the cow's benefit. Now, in comfort, she grazes protein-rich forages without the high levels of parasite infestation that once drained her body of milk- and meat-producing abilities.

In addition to grass and legumes the helpful forbs become an asset in our systems approach to livestock husbandry. The practice of true animal husbandry, almost forgotten by modern farming methods, can be realized. The farm exists as a functioning organism. No longer are we applying costly chemicals to rid the pastures of what once were improperly categorized as unnecessary weeds. Some of these forbs have the ability to reach deep below the top level of soil and bring forth nutrients missing at required levels for improved animal nutrition. The cow appears to have abilities of self diagnosis and searches out the specific plants which have medicinal capabilities for improving her digestion and metabolism.

Each time we open a fresh pasture some of the cows travel directly to the walnut trees and reach high to gather a mouthful of leaves. The reason she walks across a sod of legumes rich in protein and labors for the leaves from trees grown without our efforts, we do not know. But experience taught us to allow the cow to select her diet. We no longer pay the feed salesman for what the cow can contribute herself. For the bovine, balancing a ration doesn't require a university degree. She mainly requires less interference on our part. We must learn to use nature in our system, not constricting her abilities by forcing corporately manufactured formulas and ideas that men have manipulated, manipulation almost always brought into play by those who no longer have the insight to actually earn a living from the soil. Like the parasite that preys on the nutrient-deficient host, these purveyors of packaged products must attempt to make their living from commissions at the retail level. Our understanding of the mechanics of organic and inorganic structures need only be elementary. Application of purchased products need only to be minimal.

Animal husbandry and grass management are improved most by the passing of time; time being critical to allow nature to perform at her optimum level. Once we learn how *not* to apply chemicals and follow practices that deter protein growth — both in the form of animal meat and plant protein — the productivity of our system increases. During this passing of time we are not ignoring the nutrient levels of our soils. We know that building organic matter into humus is at the frontline of our grass management program. Raising organic matter content from below 2% to above 3% is considered an impossible task by many people. At my ranch I have accomplished this in many different pastures in as little as three years with very little cost of purchased chemical fertilizers. In some pastures organic matter now tests in excess of 7%, and I have applied nothing but herd management. I now believe most of my purchases were in vain, a partial waste of money. Managed with intent rather than with ignorance, the cow can provide a steady flow of organic, soil-building materials. The same group of cows left on the same acreage to pilfer the entire ranch at will has the guidance of a fool. In a time before fencing, this same group of cows would eat an area of ranch pasture down. With completely free roaming rights they would move off to another large grazing land and possibly leave the former pastures to rest for a full year or more. This ensured a continual regrowth of forage from year to year without depleting the organic matter in the soil. This group of cows would graze off an area of ranchland, devouring the nutrients above ground and allowing the grass materials below ground to become fodder for the process of building additional soil organic matter.

The natural process of soil restoration with decaying roots and the stomping of forage into the soil by animals' hooves is critical, a form of mob grazing by definition. This was a form of management only afforded when there were large quantities of inexpensive grassland. This ranch now is bordered by five strands of barbed wire. The cows are locked to the management which holds them in. Left to their own demise the group of cows locked into these 1,000 acres will destroy the grasses, and then the soils, and ultimately themselves. They are no longer permitted to leave the ranch for other grasses a long distance away. A small patch of grass will be eaten on each day until the root system has weakened and finally given up. Without a period of time to rest, the soil is exposed to the hot sun and the destruction of what nature built in a thousand years is accomplished in only a few short grazing periods.

To rest these pasturelands, a system of grazing management is put into place that replicates what nature can do, without the interference of poor management on what are no longer inexpensive grazing lands. The high cost to purchase grazing land for livestock is the driving force behind better grazing management. If an abundance of grazing land should become available to all ranchers, there would be little need for fencing. We would simply move our cows to different large tracts of land allowing as much as two or three years of nature's growth to replace what we had taken in the last grazing period. And in most cases the cows would move themselves along to prime grazing pastures free from fresh cow manure, urine and parasites. I contend it is therefore economics that drives poor grass management. It is also economics that drives progressive grass management in which a poorly managed cow herd can be made profitable once again. Once ignorance of nature's abilities is no longer ignored, a planned grazing system can be put into place. There is little one can do about the high cost of grazing lands, so we must fence our cattle into this 1,000-acre ranch and become nature's helper.

The interior fencing of the ranch requires great thought and a well-planned strategy for annual grazing. It is this interior fencing, sub-dividing the ranch into grazing paddocks, that will begin our process of providing resting periods for all the pastures not currently being grazed. The system of unlimited grazing on inexpensive, unlimited grazing lands must be mimicked on the enclosed ranch. The hillsides are fenced off from the creek bottoms. Cattle must not be allowed to graze the wet, soft bottom ground during the rainy or wet winter. Extended pugging over these wet soils will decrease available forage in the short run. However, after many years of experience, I have found it is this pugging or stomping of the hooves against even wet soils that helps once-dormant seeds spring to life. Thin soils on the ridges will hold up the cattle during the wet season, but the deeper soils of the creek bottoms will hold additional moisture during dry summers. Soil types are fenced in rather than geo-metrical predetermined shapes that relate not to growing pat-terns and abilities. I graze a group of about 500 cow/calf pairs on this 1,000-acre ranch today. On a typical June morning I might move these cattle into a creek bottom pasture of 15 acres. In two days the cattle have grazed over the clovers and have taken most of the remaining forage down to a height of about two to three inches. I open a gate leading to a hillside pasture and filter the cattle into a 10-acre pasture that hasn't been grazed since early spring. After only one day this pasture is in need of a rest so once again, I open yet another gate and move the cattle into the next pasture in succession. With more than 100 paddocks with sizes varying between 5 and 30 acres I am able to replicate a grazing system that once required no fencing. But since these cattle are locked into these 1,000 acres, planned grazing management is required.

Each growing season I will select a different set of paddocks to graze for only a very limited amount of time. These select few paddocks will be allowed to grow to maturity. Most forage will completely go to seed in less than 60 days, allowing for a con-tinual renewal of seed production over the entire ranch in a few years. This building of a seed bank of all the different grasses, legumes, and forbs most replicates what happens in nature. And this is all at no cost. Only the planned progression of rotational grazing with nature's abilities in the lead tallies my expense for forage. Once the grasses in these paddocks have reached extreme heights the entire herd will be allowed to graze heavily. The shock of mob grazing these tall grasses down to a much lower level will cause the root systems below ground level to die off in a planned manner. This routine, with large amounts of organic matter building material at the plant root site creates an environment for building years of organic matter in a much shorter period of time. This system of creating what happens in nature, only in a controlled area, improves efficiency in both quality and quantity of grasses grown on the ranch. All of this is done without the purchase of chemical fertilizers or other costly inputs.

3
Cow Economics 101

BEAUTY IS IN THE EYE OF THE BEHOLDER. This statement is relevant because the way we look at something is many times more important than the reality of what we are looking at. Perception can truly be our reality. From the sidewalks and streets of the suburbs, a ranch is many times viewed as merely an investment.

Some people might perceive the property that the rancher has acquired as mainly a real estate venture. After all, the closest thing they have to compare the ranch to is the process they went through to be a homeowner. When they first decided to purchase a home, they spent endless hours looking at prospective homes all over their area. They compared property tax costs, appraised values, undervalued homes, opportunities for equity building, and other factors which have absolutely nothing to do with daily living in their new home. This line of thought is provoked by a perception that modern-day people have about their homes. A home is considered, to the general homeowner, as much an investment as it is a place to come back to each day after work and raise a family. If the average home would be worthless at the end of a 30-year mortgage, I don't think we would be able to employ near as many real estate agents as we do in this country. It is this perception that buying a home is a good investment that keeps the wheels of the housing industry greased.

Similarly to most people a big, sprawling ranch is nothing more than a piece of real estate that has not yet been developed. That same line of reasoning is used by many people with the purchase of a cow. They are searching for ways to find a bargain on their purchase. The thought process is that I can increase the value of my purchase if I can buy a cow when the market is down and sell that product when the market goes back up, whenever that is. This thinking is how the mind of an investor works. One of the first rules of investing is to never invest money that you can't afford to lose. An investment, for the most part, is the potential for additional gain over and above the necessities of life. Could most people really afford losing their homes? If the value of my ranch and cattle went to zero, how long do you think I would still be able to enjoy the benefits of not having to go to work in town? The answer to that question is about two weeks after my cash runs out and the refrigerator becomes empty.

Although the value of my ranch, and maybe the value of my cows at a much slower rate, might increase over time, my daily survival depends upon much more than the increase in value of my total assets.

Ted Turner, landowner and investor in thousands of acres, may never miss the loss of a ranch here or there if values went to zero. He may very well utilize ranching as an investment tool and have the intentions of riding the bumpy ride upward with inflationary increases in land values. But chances are that his large portfolio of investments is balanced to the degree that his survival — or in his case his standard of living — is no longer affected by market swings. The average American, or rancher, will have a very difficult time maintaining a life on a ranch at all if his only strategy is to buy a cow when she is undervalued and sell her when prices go back up. This is a game for millionaires.

I am not speculating that the value of my ranch will not increase in value. I firmly believe it will easily double in value at least once every generation, if not more. This is very good for my children, if they don't want to be in the ranching business after my death. But whether my acre of grass is worth $100 or $100,000, it still produces the same amount of feed. And it is this grass that I seek to convert to a marketable and renewable product called beef that feeds my family each year. It is imperative that I am able to produce each pound of beef with a gross margin which will cover my fixed costs, my rising input costs, and have enough left over to pay for my electricity, phone bill, some groceries, etc.

If I were a savvy buyer I might be able to buy all my cows at something less than what they are worth on the market. But if each cow costs more to maintain than what her calf can be sold for at the end of the year, there is going to be a serious cashflow problem soon. This idea of buying low and selling high has no place at all in the general cow/calf business of ranching. You may get lucky a time or two, but sooner or later you will hit the market falling instead of rising, and it will all be over. This unsafe manner of buying and selling is not really agriculture at all. The synergy that should exist between a rancher and his animals has very little chance to mature when every animal on the ranch is doomed for a one-way trip to town before the year is out. The true economics of good farming stems from the learned and practiced methods of animal and soil husbandry which depend on the improvements made each successive year both in the genetics of the herd and biological improvements in his soil. This can only come about from a long-term relationship between a farmer and his farm.

The typical downward spiral we see in the condition of the rented farm is a prime example of shortsighted, greedy people. The farm is a living organism housing many organisms, with man at the top of the pyramid. When quick cash is man's first desire, the downfall of all organisms on the farm or ranch will soon occur. Profits of a farm come about because man can see and be a part of the synergy between soil, water, sunlight and plant growth. This is not something to cash in on, but is an obligation that is bestowed upon the fortunate farmer who can take only from the land the profits needed and return the balance for the good of the organism itself. The gross margin calculation may to most people be only numbers on paper, but to the agrarian it is viewed as a responsibility and a career of the highest calling. The terms *profit*, *costs* and *margins* are the only requirements for farming in a growing population that sees farmland as having value beyond its ability to produce food. We must develop the economic and financial skills which become as important to the sustainability to the farm as soil nutrition.

This gross margin I discuss is a very simple concept. It is very closely related to profit. It is another way of looking at the profit that you will receive from each unit of product that you have to sell. After overhead has been covered, take gross margin and multiply that number times the number of units (calves) you have to sell in order to determine net profit. We will not get into the complicated accounting terminology in our discussion here. For our purposes, we just need a basic structure to compute profit and loss. And remember, we must know these approximate figures to keep our enterprise of ranching alive and viable. It is this profit that enables us to feed and clothe our family each year.

If your calves are worth $500 at sale time, you must have something less than $500 in expenses (costs) to produce that calf. Once I add up interest expenses, fertilizer costs, hay purchases, fencing and wire, etc., I will come up with an amount to divide by the number of calves I have to sell each year. If this number equals anything less than $500, I have a positive gross margin. For instance, if my total cost of production equals $425 for the year, I have a $75 gross margin. If I have 300 calves to sell, I must be able to maintain my household on $22,500 ($75 x 300 calves) for the year to stay in business. This gross margin must be calculated on the number of calves you have to sell, and not multiplied by the number of adult cows you maintain. If you run 300 cows you might only have 260 calves to sell by the end of the year. You will have cows that don't breed, cows that die during the year, calves that die, and a million other possibilities that haunt all cattlemen. Therefore, when you sell a smaller number of calves per year, your unit cost will increase. No matter how many calves you sell your overhead cost generally remains the same. Therefore, it is overhead costs that must be budgeted first and paid first.

It can be very helpful when considering adding enterprises to the farm or ranch to analyze which possible new enterprise contributes the most toward covering overhead costs. Once overhead costs have been covered by the main ranch enterprise or business, other opportunities come into play. For instance, your farm payment (overhead) is the same amount each year regardless of how many calves you safely raise throughout the year. At this point you must come to the realization that the more calves you sell per cows you own the higher your gross margin will be. Reproduction of our cow herd becomes directly related to gross margin. Reproduction is the top variable for profits on a ranch. The false conclusion that many naïve cattlemen come to is that the bigger the calves are, the more dollars they will sell for; therefore, gross margin will be bigger. Along with feed costs that are out of line, this is the absolute top reason for lack of profitability in most all unprofitable cow/calf ranches in the United States today. And, of course, striving toward bigger calves is the key driver of higher and higher feed costs. Bigger calves come from bigger cows and bulls which in turn require more quantity of feed and generally a higher quality of feed, all leading to a higher maintenance cost. This in turn increases the costs of production. It is now evident that gross margin will decrease. This proof is given here by simple mathematics proven to be flawless centuries ago.

The cow is a perfect converter of poor-quality forages into market-demanded meat, or protein. She is not very efficient with other feedstuffs, like costly purchased corn and other inputs, especially when total expenses like mechanization and labor costs are included. It is forages that she is able to feed herself with very little interference from us farmers and ranchers. Generally speaking, if she has trouble producing a profitable calf each and every year on mainly what the ranch can grow, it is the selection of the cow individually wherein the first management error may have occurred. It will never be advisable to feed the cow in excess to increase the gains on the calf to unrealistic levels.

So the answer is to always buy, or raise, cows that can produce a calf for less than her own maintenance costs. And this maintenance must be accomplished on forage. This is a seemingly simple solution to the profitability of the ranching industry. It truly is that simple. One might have the perception that selecting these types of cows would be as easy as walking into any clothing store and buying a new shirt. There are cattle sales held in hundreds of towns and cities all over the country every week. Purebred ranches spend millions of dollars breeding for seedstock and many more millions to market their line of genetics. Many people — even some who have owned cattle for years — are under the mistaken idea that many of these cattle can produce a solid gross margin on their ranches.

And so we go to a reputable seedstock producer and look over his pen of bulls. We appear impressed when the owner or livestock manager brings forth a page of attributes presented mainly in the form of EPDs. Our eyes hone in on the weaning weight of this bull. We remember last year that our calves weighed only an average of 475 lbs. each. This bull weighed 950 lbs. at 205 days according to his EPD on weaning weight. We purchase this bull, take him back to the ranch, and turn him out with the cows. The following year we keep back 20 nice looking black heifers to put into our cow herd for replacements. We noticed they are much taller and bigger than heifers we've had in the past. Now we're thinking that next year's calf crop will be even bigger and our gross margin will increase, because we are certain to sell more pounds of calves after weaning time.

But to our surprise our conception rate on those new heifers was less than half of what was normal. So instead of having our expected 20 additional calves to sell, we only had nine healthy calves from these heifers at the end of the year. And these new heifers are not looking very good on our pastures; they seem to be thin. So we start a program of supplementing five lbs. of grain per head per day. Suddenly our gross margin went into the can. Our costs went up in feed and our percent of calf crop went down in relation to the number of adult cows we are feeding. It's getting close to time to breed the cows again and this new bull kind of looks like the new heifers, he seems extra thin.

The next year, when we wean off the calves, we not only don't have a calf for every heifer we raised, we have 15% fewer calves to sell from our mature cow herd. It seems to get those extra pounds on the weaned calf cost more than we expected, both in loss of reproduction in our cow herd and increased costs in feed for inefficient-type heifers. And what is really a slap in the face is that it took at least three years and thousands of dollars to learn this lesson about productivity. Plus, we've got these new genetics started in our herd, and the problem will be with us even longer. Many times this realization doesn't come to the forefront, if ever, for 10 years or more. By then gross margin is so low that we give up and go to work in town, claiming that there just is no profitability in the cow business. Many well-intentioned cattlemen walk away with their heads down wondering how wrong their thinking had been.

Quite often I hear people make statements about how much money there is in this industry or that industry. It goes something like this, "yeah, you know that computer business . . . there's a lot of money to be made in that business of computers." What a ridiculous statement to make. Most of us know that Bill

Gates has made several fortunes with Microsoft. But I have a sneaky feeling that guys like Bill Gates can make a fortune in whatever business they are in. Whoever thought there would be any money in selling twenty-nine-cent hamburgers? Someone at McDonalds must have known. What about sub sandwiches? Have you ever heard of Subway? I am here to admit that entering a new industry at its pre-ripening stage, catching the stock as it's climbing instead of when it has peaked is obviously advantageous. But the cattle business is certainly not a new, high-tech industry. I doubt any of us are going to beat the nextdoor neighbor to the punch in the cow/calf world.

So what is it that has made these other businesses so successful that we can borrow from and utilize in our cattle business? I have no doubt that these companies are run by motivated, positive thinking individuals, but I also know that the key elements of success are found in the systems that they employ. Each time Walmart opens a new store in a new location they don't have to invent a new management style. Their proven system is already in place. Every McDonalds we walk into from California to New York is set up in almost identical format. A successful organizational system is one that can be written down, repeated, duplicated, and put into practice like an exercise program.

As ranchers we are never for sure about the amount of rain we will receive in any given season. Ditto for other operations variables. But we must have a plan of action to put into place when the variations in rain, cattle prices, inputs, and other factors that affect our profitability occur. If we had a *Systems Log of Operations,* we could turn to page 246, as an example, when it doesn't rain for two months and determine what the system requires. If you return merchandise to Walmart, the local store manager does not have to call some home office to determine the procedure. This is all part of the system that has been put in place in advance. For the ranch to stay viable there must be a procedure ready to be activated with every anticipated event. The ability to have such a detailed system in place more often than not sets successful ranches apart from the ones that have been sold off and subdivided for housing developments.

By looking at the successful ranch we can see from a distance some of the factors which have to do with success. Quite often it is the things we don't see parked around the barnyard and along the edge of the pastures that affect profitability. We've discussed at length the efficiency of the cow. So why is it that we see large investments of machinery — or iron, as it is so often referred — parked mostly idle in various states of repair around the ranch?

Many times I've visited with failing cattle ranchers in depth who have more invested in their machinery and hay equipment than they do their cow herd. A wise man once said that all you need to run a ranch is a wheelbarrow. But that is only if you enjoy operating machinery. I have come up with a list of tools that seem to me to be the only necessary equipment purchases for running a cow/calf ranch. I have run a profitable ranch with very few other tools than what is listed below. After 30-some odd years of operating my ranch, I do now enjoy the convenience of a 40-year-old tractor and loader, but this extravagant purchase was made only after 27 years of ranching success, with ownership of over $1 million of debt-free cattle and land assets.

To run a profitable ranch you must have the following 10 tools:

1. Roll of poly wire with posts.
2. Wire cutters, with hammer on one end.
3. Wire stretchers.
4. Hand post driver.
5. Corner post bar.
6. A pickup truck with at least a hand wench for lifting bales of hay; most everybody already owns some sort of transportation, it might as well be a pickup truck.
7. Logging chain.
8. One 20-penny nail, or screwdriver.
9. Chainsaw.
10. The most important tool of all, a successful, proven management system.

No doubt there are additional tools that can make life easier on the ranch. I see no reason why a new startup rancher would purchase any other tools, whether small or large, until the new operation is earning a good income. Many of the tools listed are standard wares that most landowners have on hand and therefore require no additional outlay of cash. If bankers were still good ranchers, like some used to be, they would seldom lend to a new rancher any money to buy machinery not on this list until the rancher's gross margins become substantial. The ranchland itself has the potential to produce almost all that the cow will need. The cow has the ability to harvest all that she will need from the ranch. This list of tools will supply you with what you need to take care of your ranch and your herd.

In the beginning years of a new ranch three thoughts should guide your-day-to-day workload:

1. If you demand a great deal of additional inputs to get your ranch through a typical year, the system you have in place will, in all likelihood, eventually prove to be unacceptable.

2. Your ranch will not support a high-input system of management.

3. Iron is for farmers; grass is for ranchers.

You must decide early on which side of the fence you are going to operate from: are you going to be a farmer or a rancher? If you try to straddle this fence, you will be working at least part-time off the ranch until the bitter end. If you maintain a limited number of inputs other than your cows and the ranchland, you will more likely be out of the way of your cows so they can do what they do best without your naïve interference.

4

How to Keep From Failing

THERE ARE PERHAPS THOUSANDS OF BOOKS written about how to succeed in business. Success is something that will gravitate toward those who can keep from failing the highest number of times. Or maybe it could better be said that success comes to he who is able to keep failing until he succeeds. It is an *ordinary* person who can work at a job and allow another person to determine his lifestyle. That is, they will tell him how often he must show up for work, what he is required to do each day, where he shall live, and what form of lifestyle he is limited to. This is not an extraordinary life.

I myself made the decision at a very early age that I wanted to live an *extraordinary* life. I want to come and go when and where I wish. This requires financial independence, which I have achieved. This also requires maintaining financial independence from a certain point forward. This is one objective that I work at now, and will for the rest of my life on this earth. Any so-called ordinary person can achieve this financial independence. This is the tremendous privilege offered to us Americans. The term *independence* can be confused with wealth by some who find it unobtainable. I do not seek great wealth. However, I have sought financial independence as described above for many years. Many times in my youth I delayed my achievement of financial independence by searching for and yearning for great wealth. I have yet in my 50-some-odd years met a single person of great wealth who appeared to receive a high level of enjoyment from life. And in most cases this great wealth has seemed to be the main stumbling block between their happiness and sorrow. As large as this world has grown, I suspect there have been some people who can balance wealth and happiness. I simply find no need to strive toward a level of income that by most apparent signs bring no common satisfaction. If I were required to find a single true reason for great wealth it must be to help those of misfortune in this world. Again, what a burden this would place on such a simple-thinking individual as myself.

It was apparent to me that I would have to be extraordinary myself to reach this goal. The ordinary person must perform in an extraordinary manner to achieve this status on his own. This person will have to work physically harder than others around him to become extraordinary. This is something that all fit people have the ability to do. It is the person who chooses to sleep until 9 a.m., and quit at 5 p.m., and complain about being tired all the time who will never be extraordinary. Even more important than the physical labor is the mental workout that must be underway at all times to some extent toward achieving this goal. Errors of judgment, the wrong product at the wrong time or place, poor marketing, etc., are all mistakes made by extraordinary people. These are also made by ordinary persons as well. What sets the two types of people apart is that extraordinary people will learn from their actions and the actions of others and make the necessary changes and adjustments to minimize these errors in the future and carry on. And just as important is that to achieve extraordinary status one must never fail. Again, failure is only accomplished in quitting or never trying.

The act of striving for a goal is a success regardless of the level of achievement. It is entirely up to the individual to determine what level to master, to determine what success is for him. Sometimes seemingly catastrophic events create temporary anxiety and shadows of failure. Despite the frustration, the people are not failures in themselves. If learning has taken place, damage is limited and under control, extraordinary action replaces the temporary setback.

So to be an extraordinary cattleman are we doomed to hard labor 15 hours a day for the rest of our lives? Does drudgery and misery from back-breaking work day in and day out produce profitable results? My answer would most certainly be, "just about never." What at first might seem to be a contradiction must be analyzed closer.

I have a buddy who is absolutely crazy about fishing. He eats, dreams and breathes bass fishing. If he is not at work, you can count on him being in his boat on some lake somewhere casting out left and right. He despises his job. He watches professional fishermen on television and dreams of tournament fishing as his perfect career. It is slavery for him to spend eight hours on the job working. But he can fish in icy cold waters from sun up to sun down on the weekend and be happy as a lark all the while. When Monday rolls around, it is like returning to a prison cell for him. When a person is totally enthralled with their activity to the point of commitment beyond question, time and effort will have no boundaries. What would appear as a miserable condition to many fishing for hour after hour in freezing temperatures is a heavenly pleasure for him.

When I take a long pasture walk I am not just inspecting the condition of my grasses, moisture, fencing and cattle. I am mostly seeking enjoyment from being in the environment that I love best. For those of us who have found a vocation that is also our passion, we have no sense of hourly work. A day, an hour, or a week has no meaning in terms of accomplishing tasks for compensation. It is not work for the cattlemen to spend 10 hours on horseback with his cattle dog gathering cattle in 25-degree temperatures. This is his passion. It is a near tragedy when a person's life work is at odds with his passion. No matter what level of income is achieved each work week, if passion is sacrificed what would there be to gain? This continuity of labor and passion is the foundation for an extraordinary life. There is no longer a need or desire to limit oneself from his career, for his job is his fishing trip, and his joy is limited only by his physical abilities to keep up with the excitement of each day.

So in order to keep from failing at ranching we must have passion on a daily basis. If we are finding drudgery at the ranch, it could be that we are trying to force the system to work against nature, our abilities, or some other practice that is contradictory to success. We must not do what others are doing just because we are told everyone does it. And we must not fail to try simply because no one has ever done it before. Many businesses have succeeded mainly because they were able to get a jump-start on others. Once others saw the success and began to imitate, the bubble had already began to bust. The leaders had already broken through their paradigm and succeeded.

A ranch enterprise must be viewed first as a business. It is handy, and maybe somewhat more comfortable, that the rancher enjoys the daily routine of the ranch life. Some would say that you first must enjoy what you are doing to be successful. Maybe it's the other way around. It is certainly much easier to enjoy something if it is successful.

Most people would rather eat at a restaurant that is packed with people than a greasy diner with filth on the floor and cockroaches in the corners. It may not be the crowd or the opinions of all the guests in the busy restaurant that makes us want to try the restaurant as soon as possible, the crowd that has alerted us to the fact that this restaurant must be a good place to eat because of all the cars parked out front. Most of us do not enjoying being in a place where we are packed in like sardines. But the large crowd of people waiting for tables certainly alerts us to the fact that the food must be really good, or all these other people wouldn't be so eager to get in. The apparent success of the restaurant does have a psychological effect on our decision whether we want to admit it or not.

How can we be assured of success in the ranching business? We must first have a desire not only to be in business for ourselves, but we must yearn to be ranchers. If tending to cattle and other livestock in all kinds of weather, fixing fences in the rain, heavy lifting, practicing animal husbandry even when it's not fun, missing out on that really important family event because the cows got out in the road at just the wrong time, or any of the other million things that happen regularly on the ranch irritates you beyond what you can handle, then ranching may not be advisable. It is not only that you enjoy these types of activities that ensures one of success in ranching. These are important factors for success, but not the only prerequisites for financial success.

Over 90% of all new startup businesses fail, regardless of what type of product or service they provide. The small percentage of businesses that do succeed do so not soley because the owners and managers enjoy their job. Their success is due mostly to the fact that their businesses are run by people who are planning to succeed. A rancher must not only have a plan in place that handles all the drudgery that comes his way at the ranch, he must have a business plan set in place which will give him and his helpers a roadmap to follow.

It is not the type of business that determines success or failure. If that were the case we wouldn't see so many successes in so many different areas of business. Does Walmart have products that are only available at Walmart? Is McDonalds the only place to buy a cheeseburger? I think not. As a consumer we can find most any of the items available in a Walmart store in hundreds of other stores across the country. And the cheeseburger is about the most common meal we can find almost anywhere, in small towns to large cities, or even in our own home kitchen. So what is it that these types of business organizations have that makes them so extremely successful? Do they hire only people who are born to flip burgers or scan retail products at the register? Probably not.

The most common thread that these organizations have is a system in place and a plan to implement that system. You can go into most any Walmart store or McDonalds across the country and they are almost identical. If you are traveling cross country and pull into a McDonalds, you know what to expect at the counter before you even get out of your car. You know the menu is almost identical and the French fries will be exactly the same as the ones you had in your hometown. And if you need a particular product from Walmart while traveling, you will know just about what aisle that product will be stocked whether you're in New York or California. They have an elaborate system in place. The system is so complicated and the organization so large that they have systems that monitor whether or not their systems are working as they should. They have a systems approach to success. They have proven to themselves that the main ingredient for their success is that they adhere to and follow their system way of doing things. They know that their success depends on how well they carry out the daily tasks of the systems in place.

The system may differ a great deal from one business organization to the next. The specific structure of the system is not that important. Most important is that the people involved in the success of the business realize the absolute necessity of the systems approach and have a plan in place to ensure systems are followed. Does this mean that all systems work and that the only need is to follow any given system? Certainly not. I believe that it is the people that make a business successful. These successful people will succeed in whatever business they are in or in whatever proven system they manage. These people are the ones who strive to succeed and will not accept failure. It is imperative to our success at the ranch that we develop systems. These systems must be in place before the crowd hits the door. At the ranch the crowd comes in many different shapes. Sometimes the crowd can be something as routine as an unexpected icestorm. And sometimes the crowd can be an interest rate increase which might come close to doubling an input cost. If the business plan that we have in place is a systems-approach technique, we will know ahead of time what we will do in both of these situations, and other situations as well.

Refusing to fail is part of this system for success at the ranch. Refusing to do things at the ranch the way everybody else does is also part of the system. Refusing to be influenced by feed salesmen, fertilize dealers, and every new farm implement sales gimmick is critical when designing your system. Most of the cow/calf herds in southern Missouri today are hobby farms, mainly because most of the operators have given up on the idea of cattle being a profitable enterprise. These operators are operating these ranches in the same manner as their neighbors. All of their neighbors have full-time jobs to support their cow herds. Their friends and neighbors spend their holidays and weekends putting up harvested feed with farm equipment that is valued at more than their cow herds. So the hobby farmer follows suit and spends more in capital expenditures on iron and stuff in a bag each year than he will see for his calf crop.

The academic world and those who publish research data provided by the land grant university — who in addition are supported by those who promote and sell many of the modern, so-called required-for-success-inputs — have tremendous power over the average farmer and rancher. This power does not come from physical restraints or political tension. It is from something much more effective. I believe this ability to pressure others to purchase unnecessary products stems from our herd mentality. Horses in the wild, and even many domestic horses, have tremendous instincts concerning this herd mentality. Horses learn from a very early age that safety comes in numbers. The closer a horse can maintain his position toward the middle of the herd, the less likely he will be taken by the lion following the herd. Few people are willing to stay on the fringes. Many feel that if everyone else is doing this or that, all these people surely cannot be wrong. It appears safer to be in the middle like supposedly everyone else.

It is an amazing sight to watch a group of preschool children at play. If one child picks up any one of the toys in a pile, that particular toy will absolutely be the favorite of one of the other toddlers. Another toddler will take that toy away if he is able. If no one appears interested in that toy after awhile, he will discard it and go to another. We have this innate desire to stay in the herd and play with what we see others playing with. It is a challenge to accept the fact that in the cattle business, if everyone else is doing it, it is probably wrong. We must first look at the few ranches in the country that are profitable and ask why they are so. This would be a much easier task than examining all of the unsuccessful ranches, because today very few ranches are operating profitably. One of the reasons for this follows.

There is much data currently circulating about the cost of winter feed for a cow herd. There are, in addition, volumes of advertisements marketing everything from vaccinations, mineral supplements, special chemical fertilizers, harvesting equipment, etc., giving ample opportunities for the rancher to spend his hard-earned money on his cow herd. Most of these purchased items are marketed by very sharp business organizations that spend millions convincing ranchers that dollars spent on their products will decrease this growing cost of feeding cattle through the winter. The method used most widely across the country today indeed creates an ever-increasing cost of winter feeding the cow herd. Some data proves that the cost of winter feed per cow will consume 75% or more of the current commodity price of the calf she is raising. I have no doubt believing this to be true when I investigate the high cost of operating a ranch the way most of my neighbors do.

Science has given us everything we need to reduce our annual feed costs to a manageable level. The same science that the fertilize dealer promotes his product with is also available to each and every rancher, in essence, free of charge. But somehow marketing experts are able to take this knowledge of science and convince most ranchers that it must be purchased over and over again in increasing amounts to the point of unprofitability for the ranch. This does not concern the input salesman. He is aware that most farms and ranches operate as hobbies. These increased costs only create more of a tax writeoff. He is also tuned into the ever-increasing supply of suckers born each day. Why should the mineral salesman care whether your operation is profitable or not? If you go out of business your ranch will be auctioned to the highest bidder and a new and possibly more naïve cattleman will be his new customer.

This available science must be understood at a basic level by the successful rancher. Degrees and diplomas in animal science or biology have very little use at the ranch from an operational standpoint. In fact, an ever-increasing education in business management would have a much more positive effect toward improving success at the ranch level. The level of science used at my ranch would be considered elementary by university standards. The science of soil biology utilized and understood by the successful ranch manager may grow as time passes and he develops a greater interest in such things. But the understanding of building soil organic matter and the harmful effects we suffer from the destructiveness of chemical fertilizers within our soils can be understood by many students without university credentials. These students will quickly learn that building of soil organic matter and applying chemicals that destroy microbial activity are antagonistic.

The salesmen/scientists have somehow convinced the masses that we must provide to the soil elements in quantity and/or form that do not exist there by nature. They do this by providing data that show higher and higher yields can be obtained with their products, when in actuality the more we apply these products to our fields, the more our soils become addicted, like the drug addict is addicted to heroin. Then the soil becomes so lifeless that without artificial soil amendments in ever so increasing quantities, yields suffer. They then are successful in convincing us that we must mechanically harvest this yield. This harvesting is done less efficiently than by leaving the cow to do what she does best: graze. Once our neighbors have sitting in their barns shiny new tractors and hay balers, we are convinced that we must also purchase more iron lest we not be as scientific and herd bound. Then to increase yield even more — to help pay for the new equipment purchase — we apply more and more costly chemical fertilizers. Costly not only in initial price per ton, but costly to the microbial activity in our soil.

With this practice we not only destroy nature's ability to systematically, biologically produce but we also remove any possibility of profits to be earned from such a raping of the land. All this manipulation comes from the idea of artificially increasing yield. Quantity — being considered of the most importance from their marketing schemes without the benefits of sustainability — if strived for, will dry up all profits. Quality being not secondary, but not even part of the equation, dries up the benefits of quality food production for animal as well as for man. And all along what has been promoted as a benefit for the ranch by the flashy salesmen becomes a burden for the serious cattleman. This cattleman may exhaust his ranch's funds before he develops a keen eye for the charlatan that only desires to transfer wealth away from the ranch. That is the transfer of what began in the cattlemen's pocket and winds up in the pockets of marketing gurus, all the while the suffering of the cattlemen's family is shared only by the loss of the organic matter in the soils.

We are able to put this science to work in our soils without costly outlays of cash. Winter feed costs need not approach the heights stated in research done by those whom have never taken large herds of cattle through either mild or severe winter weather. The cow can graze her way through six inches or more of snow, provided forage is available at ground level. Stockpiled forages saved for winter feed in a system of rotational grazing throughout the year can provide most or all of the requirements needed of a dry or lactating cow with her calf at her side. This forage self-feeds the cattle all winter long without the need for tractors and other heavy and expensive mechanical harvesting equipment that do damage not only to the cashflow statement, but also creates hardened soils beneath its path.

Science teaches us that the atmosphere is full of more nitrogen than we can utilize. It teaches us how to build organic matter in the soil to build swards of forages for year-round grazing, even in colder climates. Nature shows those with open eyes which forages stay green even during times of drought. The planting of grasses and legumes along with forages less popular in today's agriculture, like chicory and vetch, will extend grazing time both in terms of quantity and quality of feed.

Practice rotating the cattle frequently, sometimes once each day depending on precipitation and other weather conditions. Learn how to allow a certain number of different pastures each year to grow into a more mature stage. Allow all of the pastures to eventually spend the time to produce their own seed to bank for later use. Giving a pasture a 35-day rest during the growing season will allow opportunity for deep-rooted plants to germinate, plants that might not have been seen for decades due to overgrazing. These deep-rooted plants possess root systems capable of reaching two or three feet, or even deeper, down through the hardpan of the soil. Even during times of drought these green plants have the ability to bring up nutrients which are far out of reach of the short grasses we typically see growing in pastures. These plants have abilities far superior to modern equipment. Some have the ability to help build more organic matter. Others draw nitrogen from the atmosphere, depositing it free of charge at the bank of root nodules of red and white clovers and other legumes.

Pure science at the ranch level is of little value. Some have compared ranching to the artistic fields such as drawing, painting or music. To combine useful science with nature, which is actually one in the same, through a business structure of rearing cattle is a form of art. Art implies sensitivity, creativity, and the construction of something pleasing. I could never describe a herd of cattle grazing in knee-high clover with any other adjectives. Cattle standing in knee-deep mud at the feed bunk waiting for the tractor to deliver harvested, low-quality and chemically enhanced feedstuffs with obscene traces of pesticides paints a picture I care not to look at. This second picture is not only unpleasant but can never be sustainable. The business of cattle ranching can be and is a viable enterprise. Understanding the science of soil and the building of humus by way of organic matter is critical to ranch grazing. We must acknowledge that cattle cannot be farmed. Putting a tractor into the pasture where the cow belongs is the equivalent to filling your bathtub with used motor oil. Neither will ever do the job intended. The cow will do what she does best if you will simply not get in her way. One way of learning more about what goes on in pastures is to spend time watching cows.

When we turn the herd into a fresh pasture in the grazing system we have an opportunity for learning. Some cows will seek out the youngest of the green forages. Others will head to the trees and begin eating leaves off branches they can barely reach, while they are standing on lush grasses. Some will seek out certain weeds that provide nutrients not available from the short-rooted grasses. The monoculture pasture promoted by most herbicide salesmen is counter-productive to the desires and abilities of the cow. A cow walks while she tears at the grass. When she fills up she will stand still or lie down. It behooves us as ranchers to get each cow filled up as soon as possible so she will cease the walking around and trampling of forages. She does this most effectively by grabbing at the largest mouthful each time she takes a bite. If the grass is short she will be forced to take many small bites. If the grass is thick and tall, each bite will contain more forage.

When we turn a herd of cattle out into a large pasture in a system — such as continuous grazing rather than a planned grazing rotation — the cows will create long, winding paths from one side of the ranch to the other. These grassless paths not only are contributing to soil erosion, but there is a considerable decline in available forage. Not only is the loss of forage apparent in the grassless roadway, but something much more devastating occurs. Heavy sod and pastures with good organic matter hold rainwater very well. Bare ground dries out quickly. Not only does this pathway dry out and is void of forage, but plants in close proximity of the path suffer from this drying out effect as well. As time goes on the path becomes wider and the destruction and loss of moisture in the soil increases. The simple practice of grouping our cows together in smaller paddocks with permanent or temporary fencing and rotating from pasture to pasture has the effect of an increase in forage. This increase will by no means be a small figure. I have had pastures that more than double in carrying capacity with no added cost.

A minimum of 12 separate pastures in a rotational system is required. Twenty or more pastures can double the forage produced over a continuous grazing system. One hundred pastures can eliminate the winter feeding of harvested forages on the same ranch that was at one time struggling to provide grass during the growing season. I use about 100 different paddocks all year long, even during the nongrowing season as I want to distribute manure and urine as evenly as possible all year long. Even if I run completely out of standing forage and begin feeding hay, I will still move the herd each day to a new pasture. The cost of winter feed need not be a large entry on the financial statement. When the practice of observation begins, costs once associated with the ranching enterprise that seemed a necessity will become obsolete. The chatter of the salesmen will eventually become an annoyance and aggravation no longer tolerated.

5
Feeding the World

THE PICTURE OF A HUNGRY PERSON, OR EVEN WORSE, A HUNGRY CHILD, haunts me in my dreams as well as my daytime thoughts. Because of my abundance of farming ground I feel like I am hoarding food away from those in need. How can I use what has been abundant to me my entire life for the benefit of those less fortunate? I have never been driven to earn a high level of income. But my lifelong desire of soil building has created a vast emptiness in my bank account. Soil, rich or poor, only comes attached to real estate. This lack of ability to separate the nutrient-building muscles required to produce food from the ever-increasing inflationary mule of farm ground is a stumbling block to getting starving people fed.

The richest soils of the Mississippi River Basin alongside St. Louis have been surveyed, marked, staked and taken out of food production forever. Miles and miles of acreages holding nature's richest nutrients are being covered in asphalt and concrete. These soils of depths of some three, four and more feet deep will never grow another green bean or potato for those on American soils — or the hungriest of children who would welcome even *one* small red potato a day. By developing this land that is much better suited for crops than shopping malls and large-square-footage houses of pretense, we are forever taking food away from future generations. These areas do not even make good developing projects. The soils are so deep and flood prone that expensive precautions are built into major construction sites in order to change the environment from what it was intended by nature.

During the 1993 flood I saw hundreds and hundreds of commercial structures and homes buried by the Mississippi's rising waters. After the water receded and the mass destruction finally exposed man's conflict, construction of new buildings was once again started on the same rich soils. At the cost of government-insured flood protection, and at the even higher cost of large quantities of soil nutrients being covered and lost, once again concrete, asphalt and steel took root. For a short while nature was trying to take back what man had stolen and molested. She knew that the hungry needed this soil. So nature sent the rains and filled the river. Once the banks began to overflow, natural deposits of plant foods began natures' job of replenishing what man had stolen. She began removing the structures that were in opposition to humanity by flooding waters. Potatoes and beans needed planting more than a new subdivision. How many souls can be fed with lumber and shingles?

And now, well over a decade and a half later, more soil nutrients have been covered than ever before. Even high-rise buildings now tower above shopping malls and paved streets where corn and red potatoes once grew. The leased space in any of the high-rise buildings will generate more immediate income for an investor than farming. How can anyone convince a financial guru in his BMW and three-piece suit that subsistence farming and raised beds are much more palatable along the banks of the Mississippi River than his subdivision? He will pay no attention to soil nutrients and Mother Nature. He knows he is insured. He knows the banks will lend money on high-yielding projects. He has no desire to soil test the rich bottom-ground to determine which, if any, minerals are deficient for a growing crop. He has never been inside a feed or seed store to purchase inputs for this farming ground. For him it is only dirt. It will soon be covered with investments of high-yielding returns. After this project is completed he will go down river and purchase more farms. Flood insurance will be in place and construction will begin once again.

My nightmares of hungry children become reality. I cannot compete for the purchase of these rich soils. The price of these farms that can grow crops so vast no one must ever go hungry for even a day are beyond what can be returned to the farmer in seed and labor. But when a house is constructed and paved streets with lights are planted, the speculator has plenty of return on his investment to continue. He has no concern about where his food may be produced or even what the cost may be. It has always been available to him in large quantities at prices that are inconsequential to a man with credit cards and stock portfolios. It is true that in America it is man's privilege to take financial risks for chances of monetary gains. Much wealth has been accumulated by individual entrepreneurs and corporations that report to their stockholders with news of rising stock values and annual dividends. But nowhere in the corporate prospectus does the cost of loss of soil nutrients show up. This debt the corporation owes will only be paid by the hungry and starving who not only exist in my dreams but in the nightmares of countless thousands, perhaps millions of hungry souls populated around the globe.

6
Bean Counting

FOR THOSE POSSESSING A MORE MEEK CHARACTER
and or intellectual education, a trained accountant is sometimes
irreverently referred to as a bean counter. The picture one often
visualizes when contemplating the physical appearance of an
accountant, or bean counter, is a sort of overweight, over-
stressed, slouching sort of fellow who is not too terribly good
looking. He is envisioned leaning over a desk shuffling stacks of
papers around, dressed in an outdated plaid suit, and gazing
through his very thick eyeglasses. I must stress to readers that
this is simply not the case. I have seen some very stylish accountants in my time. They do not all fit the stereotyping described
above. I should know; I am trained as an accountant and worked
in the industry years ago. During the many years I was growing
my ranch, I worked fulltime in a CPA office. I prepared income
tax returns, financial statements, consulted with clients. Not
once was I ever referred to as "old four eyes." I do have to admit

that most of us accountants do prefer numbers over people. Be assured that it's not that we don't care for people, it's just that the old saying "numbers never lie," is all so true.

I believe it is my accounting background and experience in the accounting profession that has given me a competitive advantage with the economic side of my ranch. I certainly realize the significance of financial planning, budget forecasting, and the absolute necessity for properly prepared financial statements. It is imperative to be able to observe the business side of a ranching operation from the picture drawn in an income statement. It is a must to be able to see in detail where each dollar was spent or earned throughout the year. We must be able to understand in detail what we have been spending on our operation and where exactly we have been spending it in order to make cost decisions for the upcoming financial period. These are the very basics of budgeting and cost control. Without adequate financial statements we can only hope to remember what we spent for cattle feed for the year. The details of what kind, when purchased, and how much feed, as well as all the other expenses for the year, must be retrievable in an understandable and usable form. I must know what I spent for fertilizer last year in order to analyze the effectiveness of the expenditure. Generally, what I spent last year is a starting point in preparing a budget for the coming year.

If as a rancher you have no interest in preparing a basic income statement for the year on your own, you must hire someone capable of preparing statements for you. Then you as the manager of the ranch must learn how to interpret the financial statements and use them as a tool for improving the profitability of the ranch. This is a tool every bit as important — or maybe even a little more so — than the rancher's ability to select and work with cattle for his herd. The accounting side of any business is very seldom glamorous. I would find it hard to visualize any profitable enterprise without adequate records for recording income and expenses. I suppose the only time I could even imagine an organization not requiring financial statements would be if its profits were so large that expenses were always going to remain irrelevant and that the IRS and the banker didn't exist. Since neither of these extremes has ever been in existence in my lifetime, I suggest all business owners develop at least a basic understanding of financial statements.

Most all financial statements have the same basic origin. The source document is the check register. As the year progresses you write checks for fenceposts, seed, hay, and many other expenses. You record each check you write in some sort of register so that you can maintain some kind of balance in your checking account to avoid writing hot checks. In a basic accounting system those amounts are organized by category. This can be done with pen and paper. With today's inexpensive computers and easy-to-learn software, it is made much easier through the use of a computer software program. This type of program can be used to record directly from your check register. Once all the checks have been entered, with a single push of a button multiple reports can be printed off to analyze all costs associated with the ranching enterprise, or you can inspect in detail each cost that occurred throughout the year. I strongly recommend the use of a simple accounting software program to be used on a personal computer. The process may seem very laborious in the beginning, but it soon will become as easy as building fence or giving vaccinations. The ability to go to the computer and look at the detail of your expenses for last year compared to this year is the best indicator of what needs to be done before we get to the point where we don't have enough money from calf sales to pay the bank note.

Once we have our financial statements prepared and take time to look at the detail of our expenses and income, we need to look at each expense as a percent of income. To get to the bottom of the barrel on this point, think about all your calf sales for the year as one big sale where we end up with one number. This number represents the total dollars we have to spend on all the expenses that might occur during the year. In almost all cattle operations the amount spent for feed will be the largest figure. I like to look at feed cost frequently. I know that if I can keep my total feed cost to less than 50% of my calf sales, I might be able to stay in business at least another year. We can learn to look at all of the other expenses in this same manner. If I spent 5% of my total calf sales on seed last year, I might set that amount as a base number for comparison. If seed cost suddenly jumped to 15% during a given year, I know that something is wrong. It is by the careful comparisons of costs illustrated on the financial statements that we as business managers are able to keep costs under control. We must know what these costs are in order to control them. Our memory is simply not good enough. These seemingly uncontrollable risks and costs have the greatest capacity to sink us. If we can learn to effectively control our costs through analysis of financial statements, we can at least minimize some of the risks we encounter on the ranch.

7

Fencing the Grass

ONE OF THE SINGLE BIGGEST CHANGES A RANCHER can make to increase the production of his operation is to put up some fences. This is seldom mentioned in the marketing blitzes of today's sophisticated animal science product sales companies. Most modern texts on livestock management place a great deal of emphasis on consumable products that must be purchased again and again on a regular basis. However, practically every feed store, hardware store, or farm and home outlet sells some kind of fencing materials. Many quality fencing materials will have a lifespan of over 20 years. It is common knowledge that cattle must be fenced. The point must be made that in fact, we are not doing fence work to keep cattle in the pastures. We are fencing in order to keep cattle out. If this raises questions in your mind, simply go to the trouble of planting a vegetable garden in the bottom pasture without putting up a fence between the cattle and your cabbage. The fence does the most good for the garden when the fence is around the garden instead of around the cattle.

So, since we know we have to do only minimal fencing, the marketing gurus in corporate agriculture try to sell us everything *but* fencing to increase our production — or their sales. We can purchase additional seed, weed killers, expensive and destructive salt-chemical fertilizers, genetically modified varieties of plants claiming to yield beyond expectations, etc. We can then borrow money to purchase tractors and other farm implements to apply these additives, these practices costing us not only the purchase price of the machinery, but repairs and maintenance and additional interest on the borrowed money and the time and labor extended to accomplish these modern marketing miracles. Many of these purchases create return and repeat business for the salesmen.

It is extremely puzzling for even the most seasoned rancher to first accept the reasons how and why a few erected fences can produce more forage without expending sums of money for some kind of extra ingredient or soil amendment. We have all learned, both in high school and college physics, that matter does not appear from thin air. It only changes form. When we place water in the freezer it becomes ice for iced tea. When we burn firewood in the wood stove it produces heat. We are only changing the form of the matter used. How can putting up a few fences create matter (more grass)? I'll admit at first thought this concept seems as if we are trying to create something out of thin air. And in a way, that is exactly what we are doing. However, that thin air is also matter. We are going to better utilize the energy from the sun, the energy that comes out of the back of the cow, the energy from rainfall, the nitrogen in the atmosphere, nutrients locked up in the soils, and recycled minerals gained by the stomach of the cow, the carbon from the trampled forage, etc.

It is the destructive nature of the cow that can be her own demise. If left to continuous grazing, the cow will first select the most desirable plants. Taking only desirable plants below a productive height of grazing weakens the structure of that plant.

This enables the less desirable plants greater opportunity to expand into the limited space of all plants in the pasture. While these more desirable and productive plants decrease in number and quality the less desirable plants, weeds and woody species encroach and thrive. Eventually the pasture sward declines to a level that not only produces less quantity of forage, but also less in quality of feedstuffs for what cattle remain. In addition, the cow under this type of management will defecate and urinate in concentrated amounts in a limited space over and over again. These large amounts of cow pies will act as a souring agent for an area several feet in diameter that the cow will not eat close to. This not only reduces grazing area, but we are also losing the tremendous natural benefit of the free fertilizer coming from the back end of the cow. The nutrients excreted by the cow on pasture are important to the ranch's fertility program. This manure and urine is by no means agricultural waste. We must learn to treat these products as the desirable inputs to the overall production of the ranch that they are.

I can take a drive through my county and find many farms and ranches with piles of wasted manure stacked up leaching out valuable nutrients into runoff water in turn entering streams and damaging the unintended. These same ranches will be purchasing nitrogen, phosphorus, and other soil amendments from fertilizer plants in a very inefficient form. They will pay large amounts for the purchase of that product and then spend more spreading unnatural and less effective forms of what they set aside to watch run off of their grassless fields.

Why is it that my county in southern Missouri boasts a population of many productive farmers yet most farmers' wives purchase their green beans at the supermarket? Most farmers in this country have become less productive and efficient instead of more so. Even with the hype of modern technology, today's farmer is more dependent upon others for his survival than possibly ever before in history. Monoculture and mono-animal agriculture has drained the farmer's brain of common sense.

This type of animal agriculture is no longer financially feasible, if it ever was.

The cow can give back most of what we need to improve the productiveness of our pastures by returning essential nutrients to our soils. Our role is to manage her footsteps so those nutrients can be best utilized. Just like the farmer's wife now buying groceries for the household from the supermarket instead of in her own garden where the savings and the quality are superior, we have given into the wasteful practice of purchasing soil nutrients at the "farm supermarket" from the fertilizer salesman because we have forgotten how to manage our cows.

Nature has her own way of returning nutrients back to the earth in order to continue a cycle of healthy soils and pastures. Prior to the 20th century buffalo herds in huge numbers moved across the Great Plains and the Midwest. These large animals with destructive hoof action would forage in a new area daily. I have read from journals of that period that the buffalo herds were so large you could look as far to the left, and then as far to the right, and then ride horseback for days through the center of a herd before you would see the borders of the herd. There is one writer who claims the herd was so fierce when they hit a locomotive from the side the train was completely lifted off the tracks and turned over. These herds moving by the thousands and tens of thousands would take out all the plant life, including weeds, and woody species in their path. By nature they would leave behind a great amount of soil-building nutrients. They would take most all vegetation, consuming some and trampling into the soil what was left, but they could not take the valuable bank of seeds in the ground. The action of their pounding hooves would aerate the soil and create the perfect environment for the rebuilding of a quality pasture sward of grasses and forbs. These herds were in the business of sequestering carbon long before carbon credits were created.

There were no fences to keep those buffalo contained. The particular pasture that was renovated by the herd would not be visited again during that season by this massive herd of animals.

This consistent moving of the herd from one area to another allowed nature to improve the forage for the herds it supported. Nature was in a way fencing the buffalo out of a pasture for a required time. It was instinct that kept these enormous herds of animals grouped together for protection from predators. But it was the temporary annihilation of the forage that required the herd to move on and not return until nature had restored and improved the conditions for new growth. No one was fencing anything in. And this is what we must emulate with our modern fencing. We will create a fencing scheme to fence the cattle out of the pastures, not to fence them in. We have learned that it is rest, most of all, that rebuilds soil and its nutrients. We can allow cattle to eat a pasture into the ground with no damage at all if we give that pasture adequate rest. In fact, this practice of decimation and reclamation over a period of time produces higher quality and more abundant forage than any other known method of sward production.

Most ranchers in North America practice continuous grazing. They dump a given number of cattle into a pasture until the grass is gone and then begin feeding hay. This set stocking requires very little, if any management, and the sorry results prove we get what we deserve. In this kind of grazing the cow is constantly on the move. She will walk mile after mile killing a large amount of forage with her heavy hoof action. First she will make a pathway across the pasture and travel that road until it is solid dirt and rock. Over a period of time these pathways will wind in and around every pebble, briar patch, watering hole and grass hopper that stays put for any length of time. These pathways will become void of all vegetation. Next, erosion will begin its dirty work, and soil and its nutrients will begin washing away with the rainwater.

The cow will select the vegetation she likes best and eat it out of existence first. She will then eat what she sees as less desirable. The manure she leaves will be concentrated in a few unpleasant areas and piled up to a point where very little use is made of what could be a highly productive soil amendment. With little chance for the grass to get ahead, for the reasons mentioned above, the quantity and quality of forage will decline very rapidly. Soon the productivity of the entire pasture will drop to one-half to one-third as efficient at growing forage as it once was.

The alternative to continuous grazing is to have some kind of planned grazing program in place. There have been several names applied over the years to this style of grazing. Some names used are "rotational grazing," "management intensive grazing," "controlled grazing," etc. In Andre Voisin's book *Grass Productivity* he refers to this type of grass management as "rational grazing." This type of system is not a modern invention. I have read books written prior to the 20th century promoting a system of grazing where the livestock, including different species (i.e. cows, sheep, pigs, etc.), are allowed to graze the sward down to a minimum height and then are taken to a new pasture. In many ways a planned rotational grazing system is more high-tech than what is practiced today in most of North America. There is very little thought and knowledge put into a grazing system that simply dumps a herd of cattle out onto a farm or ranch and lets them do what they care to on their own accord.

For a rotational grazing program to be successful, knowledge of various grasses, legumes and forbs and their growth patterns must be understood. A pasture of 40 to 50% legumes can help sequester most of the nitrogen needed from the atmosphere to feed the leguminous plant, and all its companion grasses as well. Without a good legume mix in the pasture sward, forage production will have a difficult time ever reaching a successful level.

When we allow the cow to repeatedly eat down the growth of a sward below one inch, without long-term rest periods, we are removing any chances of having a quality forage or any other significant percent of legume in our pastures. As the cow grazes she will naturally eat these high-protein legumes first. Grasses tend to grow in a more upward reach, as compared to the legumes that tend to cover the ground, more like a vine-type plant would. By taking some of this growth away, the sward is opened up to a more efficient growth pattern.

Because the cow is a much better chemist than any of us could aspire to be, she will consume an appropriate level of grasses, legumes and forbs to balance her diet and add fiber. She will also find required nutrients in the deep-rooted forbs, which some continuous grazers call weeds and apply poisonous herbicides to eliminate. Agriculture fundamentally is the building and nurturing of life. All things ending in *-icide* have to do with death, *i.e.* herbicide, pesticide, fungicide. I urge everyone in the *nurturing* business of agriculture to resist these forms of death and "suicide." During the growth period, which begins in southern Missouri around late March, the rotational grazing program moves into a higher gear. This is the time we may choose to use forward grazing, moving the herd forward into several different paddocks perhaps three, four or more times a day. Grass is growing very rapidly during this time. How we manage this growth now will have a great deal to do with our production, usage of the forage, and its relationship to winter feed costs as well.

It is impossible to discuss a planned rotational grazing system without being specific about size of pastures. The hard truth is that the size of the pasture is directly related to the aimed for efficiency coefficient. If we chose to continuously graze our herd, our efficiency might be in the range of 30 or 40%. If we split our ranch up into six different pastures of 100 acres each and chose to rotate through these pastures for one week each, we might improve to an efficiency level of 50 or 60%. On the other hand, if we were willing to move our herd into a fresh paddock every six hours and compound a stock density to a level of maybe 100,000 lbs. or more of cattle per acre our efficiency would soar and benefit from the use of 20 or 30 different paddocks. Of course, this type of rotational grazing would require additional labor to move the cattle. In this type of intensive program we may have very few pastures larger than five acres in size. We could be running 300 or 400 head or more cattle in one group through our rotation. A term that some use for this form of grazing is "mob grazing."

I have used mob grazing here on my ranch and it has proven to be the most productive method of grazing. We soon become much more in tune to the production of our pasture sward than ever before. We soon realize that production efficiency comes not as much from the breed or color of the cow as from growing legume-rich pastures that require very few outside inputs beyond the rotation of the herd. The level of efficiency that a rancher is willing to operate at will lie somewhere between these extremes. I am of the opinion that with proper management and adequate time for soil improvements an efficiency rating of over 80% could be achieved.

During our April-May growth period our pastures are growing at their peak performance here in the Midwest. We need to turn cattle into each pasture as it reaches about six to eight inches in height and eat that sward down to one or two inches. During this peak growth period this can be a challenge. By getting out into our rotation as early as possible, our chances are increased best. Once the hotter temperatures of summer arrive and our largely cool-season grasses slow their growth, our rotation slows as well. Early on we make an attempt to get all the good we can out of this rapid, quality growth and try our best to keep as many pastures as possible eaten down below two inches. This is generally not possible in every pasture on the ranch. We will at this time take a certain number of paddocks out of the rotation in order to do a better job with the remaining paddocks. The paddocks that were taken out of the rotation during the growth spurt will be stockpiled for later use.

Many ranchers feel it practical to mechanically harvest some of the excess growth. Because of the high cost of machinery and labor, I do not feel this is feasible. However, a middle-of-the-road practice of hiring a neighbor with his hay equipment can sometimes be beneficial. It is a common practice in New Zealand, where rotational grazing has become the norm rather than the exception, to use custom harvest companies to make the rounds of the many farms and ranches and perform this service. This is not now the case in North America. If and when we are able to benefit from such a service here in the United States, I feel it would certainly be worth investigating thoroughly.

It becomes a challenge, if not impractical, to perfectly match the growth of the sward with the feed requirements of the herd throughout the seasons. Not only are the seasons' changes affecting growth, but the variation in rainfall and temperature within each season from year to year may vary a great deal. For some stocker operators varying the carrying capacity of the ranch may have some effect, however with most cow/calf operations the herd size is static. It is generally only during droughts that a rancher will resort to herd reduction. Again, we are striving to have the most efficient grazing system we can make work with what resources we have available at the time. Our level of efficiency will certainly vary from year to year and from season to season. But it is our persistence at keeping the herd moving at a pace set by the growth of the sward that will improve our level of performance most.

When a rancher makes the move from another system to managed grazing he will generally begin slowly with a subdivision of his existing pastures into smaller-sized paddocks. I have found that with my current herd size of 400 cow/calf pairs, I prefer 10-acre paddocks. Some of the paddocks may be only three or four acres, and some are 30 acres in size. It seems that as the years go by I have a tendency to keep shrinking each paddock smaller and smaller. This is mainly because as time goes by I see more and more efficiency with smaller and smaller pastures. There are times when I simply don't feel like moving cattle quite as often; I want to goof off for a few days and ignore the cattle. In these cases I might open the gates to more than one pasture at a time. Again, we as individual managers must decide how efficient we want to be.

With the shrinking of each paddock comes the need for additional water sources for each new paddock. This generally requires more upfront labor and investment.

I prefer as many natural water sources as possible. If I can deliver water into a new paddock that is not sourced from well-water, I will. I much prefer spring developments and pondwater as water sources. Our hills and hollers are seeping with water if you know where to look. These dripping water sources are sometimes almost completely hidden to the casual observer. The ability of the cow to perform on drinking rainwater should be on our minds when high-quality drinking water for man becomes as scarce as it has become in many parts of our country.

Many times a good water source for a spring development may only appear to be a soft, wet place under a sycamore tree overhanging a few rocks. Generally after 30 minutes to an hour with a backhoe what was at first a squishy, spongy area becomes a catch basin for a spring development. Once the backhoe locates the water source — generally only a few feet from where the water appears on the surface — I lay down a section of four-inch pipe with drilled holes every three inches or closer. Drain fill pipe works well. This perforated pipe becomes my collection tank. I then connect this collection pipe to as many feet of pipe necessary to reach a tire tank, concrete tank, or whatever type of cattle drinking facility I desire. I backfill the collection pipe with gravel so the spring water can filter down into the drilled holes. I can use a single spring for one tank or connect several tanks in a row through several different paddocks. This system, being all gravity-flow and requiring no power, is freeze-proof and requires little maintenance.

My second choice is a gravity-flow water system developed from dug ponds. Many times a single pond can service several paddocks below with buried waterlines connected to concrete troughs or tire tanks. I choose not to have portable water tanks that I have to follow the cattle. Even though this is commonly practiced in my area of the country, I do not want the extra labor of constantly moving water tanks every time I move cattle. I do have a few waterlines connected to the three wells on my ranch that feed several paddocks. But this always concerns me because of my lack of trust in the weather and our utility company, as well as my reluctance to depend on technologies such as electricity and water pumps. Many times it is the added cost and trouble of putting in new water systems that prevents sectioning of more paddocks. This is a problem that must be addressed on each ranch. The cost of more water will surely return premiums in additional forage as time goes by. We must learn to fence water into each paddock when at all possible. This can best be accomplished when we accept that very few if any of our paddocks need be kept in perfect squares, rectangles, etc. The source and location of the water source will have a great effect on the layout and shape of each paddock.

Fencing cattle out is the goal when laying out a rotational grazing system. Continuous grazing is just about the most inefficient system to feed cattle. Each pasture must be given ample growth time to allow white clover to become significant. With continuous grazing only the more dominate tall grasses will succeed. And even they will be starved for nutrients, limiting production. If we can learn to utilize the white clover as a leading indicator other legumes and quality forbs will appear in our pastures almost magically. In most cases white clover, red clover, alsike clover, lespedeza, alfalfa and other legume seeds are already in the soil to some extent. We must give the pasture sward an opportunity to show us what is already there. Those seeds, and many others, have been put there over a long period of time. Previous operators have planted many different types of grass and legume seeds at many different times. Your neighbors have planted these seeds as well. Birds and other wildlife have unknowingly lifted seeds from your neighbors and have scattered them across your pastures. Most of the seeds lie dormant for years and years. They wait patiently for the conditions for germination to come about. The dominate tall grasses and the unmanaged cow herd of continuous grazing will not allow those seeds to grow to fruition.

By grazing a small paddock's forages down to a height of one or two inches and then moving the cattle to the next paddock in line, we open up the canopy for energy, sunshine — to reach some of those seeds. These seeds may have been waiting for years and years for this opportunity. At first there may only be a small amount of germination of legumes. As we continue our rotation we make available more energy from the sun, deposit more cattle excretions, and offer more disruption of the soil surface by hoof action. By rotating through each paddock, even the ones with limited forage, we are beginning a process of rejuvenating each paddock. The cost of this process is only inexpensive electric fencing to keep the cattle out while the process of germination and soil improvement has a chance to begin. This is called rest. The change in pasture sward will be noticeable in the very first season. The improvement to the soil and grasses growing there will be exponential.

We will see many new seedlings after a very short amount of time, generally white clover being the dominant legume — and most sought after. Without any form of cultivation we can add to our mixture of grasses, legumes and forbs to further complement the sward. This can be done most effectively and efficiently in late winter while the ground is still freezing and thawing. On a small scale, broadcasting seed on top of the ground can be accomplished with a cyclone seeder strapped across your shoulder. Large parcels of land can be seeded in the same manner with a larger unit mounted on the three-point of a tractor, four-wheeler or bed of a pickup truck. The goal is to get a broad variety of grasses, legumes, herbs and forbs established into the sward. Additional seed can be broadcast in the manner above for minimum labor and only the cost of seed. I like to think my broadcasting of additional seed as a supplement to what seeds and plants already exist in the sward. By physical observation I can see what is missing in each paddock and make changes according to what I want the pasture to look like.

This flies directly in the face of modern monoculture practices. We have become accustomed to seeing, either in photographs or advertisements, or may have even been taught, what a productive pasture should look like. A manicured golf course or homeowner's lawn has only one primary goal, and that is generally to get rid of all species save one type of grass. This practice has overtaken our farm ground as well. This is done with costly herbicides, pesticides and chemical fertilizers. This monoculture is not only expensive, but not very appealing to the herbivore. And it has become part of a very large inefficient farm plan. We must learn to retrain our eyes as to what is appealing to us as well. A well-maintained golf course may have swayed our opinions about what is beautiful in a pasture. It has certainly planted an incorrect image in our minds of what we should strive for in a pasture for cattle.

A quality pasture must have biodiversity to approximate the needs of the grazing animal. A variety of grasses, legumes and forbs must be present to meet the needs of the cow during each season of the year. Some legumes like white clover respond well for several months of the year once the growing season begins. These lower growing plants must have space and not be crowded out by the heavy canopy of taller grasses. Others, like red clover, lespedeza and alfalfa, grow to a taller height and are much more drought tolerant. Few grasses compare to tall fescue for winter hardiness and stockpiling abilities. The deep-rooted forbs like chicory or late-season vetch not only stretch the growing seasons, but these and many others can bring up rich nutrients from the soil that shallow-rooted plants cannot. Monocultures do not exist anywhere in nature. Neither is there a place for monoculture on a cattle ranch. The biodiversity from a pasture sward of mixed grasses, legumes and forbs is essential to the productiveness of the bovine and required for the economical sustainability of the ranch.

This mixture of seemingly endless variety in the pasture sward is never constant. It changes daily along temperature, the amount of energy from the sun, the seasons, and even changes in soil nutrition brought about by rotating cattle through the pastures. Therefore, to demand a certain percentage of any given species of grasses, legumes or forbs would be ludicrous. Only approximate percentages of each can be assigned for discussion purposes. For most pastures I prefer about 65% legumes available, with the dominant clover being white clover. I have broadcast many different grasses, legumes, herbs and forbs to increase the existing biodiversity in the paddocks. I have had success with the following mixture when seeding new ground for the first time.

Variety	lbs./acre
Kenland red clover	3
Ladino clover	1
Alsike	1
Alfalfa	2
Red River crabgrass	1
Chicory	2
Kentucky 31 fescue	5
Orchard grass	5
Hairy vetch	1
Kentucky bluegrass	5

This mixture is by no means exhaustive or magical. I have used many variations of this mix and other seeds that are not mentioned. I want to see the grasses mentioned in this mix in all my pastures during some time of the year to some degree or another. For the paddocks reserved for winter strip grazing, I prefer a much higher concentration of fescue. Fescue holds up to winter conditions better than any other grass I have used. Fescue actually becomes of higher feeding quality as the winter progresses. It is entirely possible to supply almost all the nutrients required by the cow all year long on a good sward of these and other grasses, legumes, herbs and forbs.

The obscene practices of monoculture and feeding large amounts of mechanically harvested feedstuffs can and must be avoided for the good of the cow and the sustainability of the ranching enterprise. By fencing the livestock out of most of the paddocks for 21 days or longer at varying times of the year, we begin the process of building biodiversity in our swards that is the foundation for making our farms and ranches to become profitable. Once our management can eventually progress to a point of grazing each paddock only two or three times a year, our efficiency rating would be very high. A very advanced grazing system might even graze each paddock only one time a year. This would obviously require about 365 paddocks.

Just as there is no precise mixture of grasses in the sward that is perfect for all occasions and all ranches, the same is true for paddock size and number of paddocks. We know here at the Rockin H Ranch that for good biodiversity in our pastures the more often cattle pass through a paddock and the less amount of time the cattle spend in that paddock — and the longer the rest period — the more grass we have available. Because of the amount of rainfall, temperature changes, sward condition, etc., our rotation can never be static. The time each pasture must rest for regrowth changes constantly. Five or six days would be the maximum time to allow the cattle to stay in any one paddock. We have found that during high-growth times of the year moving cattle twice a day is most beneficial. It is during this time of the year — with at least daily moving of the cattle from one paddock to the next — that in a very short amount of time we have excess pasture. This is even the case when the same number of cattle on the same ranch created a short supply of grass before the system was initiated.

Once rotational grazing is put into place in a short amount of time the problem changes from grass being in short supply to having a supply of enough cattle to handle all the grass being produced. This is a much better problem to deal with than the former. I have found that acquiring additional animals in the form of yearlings to graze excess forage can be part of the solution. These animal numbers can be adjusted during different times of the year depending upon the growth of the grasses. Increasing adult cow numbers too much can become a problem when drier weather arrives or conditions become less than optimal. This can lead to the selling of good-quality seedstock at a time when the market may not be favorable. In addition, I have found a tremendous benefit in planning my calving dates as the extra pasture growth correlates directly with larger calf sizes. By calving part of my herd in the fall, my calves are big enough in the spring to utilize some of that excess growth due to the spring rains and good growing conditions during that time of year. The practice of mechanically harvesting the excess growth is practiced by some. But I emphatically caution those who choose this strategy because of the large investment in machinery and labor. The purchase of machinery to utilize excess growth is like buying a bank to hold your valuables. It would be very easy to have more value tied up in the bank building than what the vault contained.

Once the ranch begins to produce this excess pasture, other opportunities and options come about. One of those options is to consider keeping some of the weaned calves over into the yearling stage. Whatever choices are made to utilize this excess forage, it is much easier to deal with than not having enough grass for the cows to begin with.

A little simple math can be helpful when estimating the desired number of paddocks. If we choose to move our herd once each day and we want 30 days of regrowth to take place in each pasture before entering that paddock again, by default we must have at least 31 different paddocks to rotate through. Since all paddocks will not contain the exact same amount of land or the same amount of forage per acre, we must be willing to adjust the stay in each paddock to compensate. We must also be versatile in the number of paddocks. This is done best by utilizing temporary fencing as well as semi-permanent fencing. I use the word semi-permanent because the high tensile wire and insulated posts that will make up most of the dividing fences can be relatively easy to relocate if needed. The perimeter fencing is fixed, and therefore the type of fencing used is not critical to our planned grazing system in most cases. At times it can be beneficial to transport the electrical current down the line of a perimeter fence via the use of offset clips and high-tensile wire in order to reach a grazing cell on the other side of the ranch. But it is the use of high-tensile wire and insulated posts that will make up the majority of the fencing around the paddocks.

Provided water is available, each paddock can be further subdivided on a temporary basis using poly wire stored on a retractable and geared reel for convenience. Insulated step-in posts are used in this case. A reel of poly wire and a handful of posts can be carried across a pasture and erected in a number of minutes by anyone familiar with the system — even a son or daughter at the age of 10 or 11. Of course with your own children this becomes as natural to them as keeping their room cleaned. I have been able to leave my 14-year-old daughter in charge of our 1,000 head of livestock to rotate through the grazing system while her mother and I are away for several days in a row.

Even though the poly wire and step-in posts allow the most flexibility in paddock size, it becomes apparent very early on that opening a new gate and closing it once the cattle come into the pasture is much easier. If our tasks for the day are made easier, we are more likely to do them with a smile and do them more often. And with growing forage we have learned that the more times we are willing to move the cows, the more forage we can grow. The point is that high-tensile and poly wire gives us great flexibility at a minimum cost compared to traditional fencing materials.

Since we estimate single-day stay periods and 30 days of regrowth time per paddock, we know we will require about 30 different paddocks. If we have a 300-acre ranch with 30 different paddocks, by interpolation each paddock would equal 10 acres. If each paddock contained 2,700 lbs./acre of dry matter pregrazing and we wanted to leave a residue of 1,200 lbs./acre of dry matter post-grazing, we would have available for grazing 1,500 lbs./acre of dry matter. We estimate a 1,000-lb. cow requires about 30 lbs. of dry matter per day. With the aid of a calculator we can see that a 10-acre paddock can feed about 500 cows for a day. A little more calculation and we come up with the fact that we are at a stock density in that paddock at 50 cows to the acre.

For those who have practiced continuous grazing, some readers just threw this book across the room and got back on their tractors. Running 50 cows to the acre may appear ridiculous to you at this time. I can remember years and years ago when I would have felt the same way, but wait just a minute. We are talking about stock density; we are not talking about carrying capacity. Stock density is the number of animals in a paddock at a particular time. Carrying capacity is the number of animals the ranch will support for the year. Our stock density in the paddock under discussion might be 500 head today, but our carrying capacity for the ranch during the full year may be 200 head. Hopefully those of you who discarded my book have picked it back up for another read. With these numbers in mind we have a carrying capacity on this ranch of 1.5 acres per cow. This is very doable in my part of the country under a grazing management program.

Under most continuous grazing systems in my area the average ranch requires about seven acres per cow. At current land prices this carrying capacity is not sustainable. We have seen carrying capacities improve to a level of as much as .7 acres per cow. That is down from having seven acres for every cow to the ability to carry over 400 cows on a ranch that before was feeding only 70 cows, by the state average. I know of grazing dairy farms that are netting $1,000 per year per cow per acre. Even if what I propose seems utterly unobtainable, if by changing your grazing management you could only double your carry capacity on your ranch, or in essence cut your expenses in half, wouldn't this be beneficial? In reality, going from a continuous grazing system to a managed grazing plan, doubling carrying capacity can be done by most everyone in a very short amount of time.

Getting back to the size and number of paddocks, the fact remains that we must remain versatile. Rainfall and other weather changes almost daily; in turn the growth of our forage is always changing. A stock density of 50 cows to the acre is quite low compared to the practices of an experienced grazier. The term *mob grazing* was introduced to the United States by an African by the name of Ian Mitchell-Innes. Mob grazing replicates what occurs in nature for the continuation of forage growth for large herds of animals. Throughout history, large herds of livestock have been free to move about the continent at will. These large herds would move in tightly knit groups for safety from predators. These large herds of thousands or tens of thousands of hooves would aerate the soil and demolish whatever forage was not eaten as the herd moved through. As the herd ate and trampled one forage area, it would move on to the next leaving behind urine and droppings for soil nutrition. This heavy stomping would rid the area of brush and woody plants which would otherwise quickly grow back with grasses and other forages for livestock. By the time the large herd made its way back through the region, regrowth would be lush.

Our planned grazing system using many different paddocks mimics this mob-style foraging. Therefore, we have learned that the more cattle we can mob up together in each small paddock the better. We can mob graze with 100 to 400 cows or more per acre and improve efficiency. By turning 100 cows into a two-acre pasture for 24 hours we can extend the amount of time that that pasture can be left for regrowth and increase total grass production for the ranch. If that pasture had 1,500 lbs./acre of usable forage, at 30 lbs. per cow we would know we had enough grass for the day in that paddock. Of course we never want to limit the forage intake in a paddock and some excess forage calculation is always safe.

In the book *Greener Pastures on Your Side of the Fence*, Bill Murphy illustrates the plant regrowth curve better than most. The three stages of regrowth are as follows:

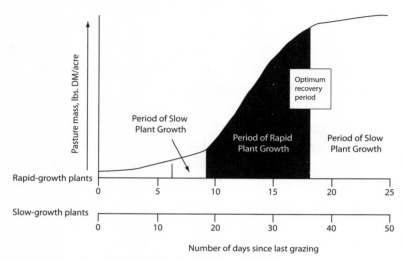

Stage 1 — early period of slow growth.
Stage 2 — middle period of rapid growth.
Stage 3 — final period of slow growth.

On a graph an S curve is created when these growth patterns are plotted. When grasses begin their growth from a height of less than 2 inches, a minimal amount of leaf area is available for photosynthesis. This early regrowth stage is a slow period of growth. If animals are allowed — as in a continuous grazing system — to eat this short growth, the plants will never reach the next stage of rapid growth and the amount of total forage will be severely limited.

As the plant reaches heights of above 2 inches the middle period of rapid growth takes hold. This is the stage where monumental growth of a rotational grazing system outshines all others. Once plants reach a height of above 8 inches, they go into the final period of slow growth.

If we are able to keep a large amount of our pasture swards at a height below 8 inches and above 2 inches for as much of the year as possible, our production of grass, legumes and forbs becomes almost immeasurable. This is one of the reasons why those who set aside large parcels of pasture ground for mechanical harvesting actually produce less forage than the grazier. Most operators will harvest hay only after it reaches a more mature stage. That is, they will harvest somewhere in the third stage of growth or later when the sward has been growing at a reduced rate for some period of time. If we chose to graze this land we will have rotated through the sward a couple of times, or more during the second stage of rapid growth.

We move cattle into a paddock at a sward height of 6 to 8 inches on average. The pasture should be eaten down to about 1 to 2 inches for an even clipping of the sward. If the paddock appears very uneven, if there are many clumps of grass across the field after the cattle have left for their next paddock in the rotation, we know stock density is too low. This remaining forage will be wasted as it will mature and the cattle will not want to eat it the next time they pass through. If this continues, weeds, brush and other woody species will eventually take hold and interfere with forage production. This does not indicate that we have not accomplished a great deal as far as growing forage and improving efficiency. It only means that we have further efficiencies yet to gain.

If we have fenced our ranch with 30 semi-permanent paddocks with high-tensile wire, we can further tweak the system with additional similar-type paddocks and/or utilize portable step-in posts and polywire within each one of these paddocks. We no longer must concern ourselves with attempting to make our farms and ranches look like golf courses. In fact, that type of practice can interfere with efficiency.

If we are using a rotary cutter or herbicides to fend off brush, we are also killing or reducing forage at the same time. Most herbicides that affect woody species also kill legumes. When we remove most of the brush on the ranch, we reduce the number of pollinators and birds that help us reseed and produce more forage. Once we initiate a planned grazing system we will see an almost immediate increase in forage. At the same time there may be a need to allow additional brush and weeds to temporarily increase to allow the other grasses, legumes and helpful forbs get a start. The idea must be abandoned that all fencerows must be free of brush. Nature has provided a great supply of free helpers to improve the conditions of our forage, soil and water. If we recognize these as partners rather than enemies, we are the ones to benefit.

I am always amazed when I see a neighbor bulldoze an old fencerow, taking out every tree and all leafy substance in order to put in a new fence. By the time summer comes around every cow on his place is standing in the pond trying to cool down because their owner took away all the shade trees. It is even sillier when he spends money on portable shade shelters and drags them all over his pasture compacting the already hard soil even further with the weight of a 150-horsepower tractor.

We must become astute at observing how nature survives without destruction. And we must learn to avoid listening and acting on the advice marketing gurus advertise in every magazine and paid advertisement. It can be as simple an act as opening and shutting a gate that moves us from a poverty-starved cow herd to a well-nourished cash cow.

As we move through our rotation each year we will have some paddocks that we are not able to keep up with. Some paddocks will simply outgrow others and we will have excess forage. This should be part of the overall plan of grazing. Each year we need to allow different paddocks to grow their forage to a mature height. Many of these forages will make seed, and some seed will fall to the soil. Birds, pollinators and other insects have the ability to transport some of these seeds to other parts of the ranch. This is one reason why we see certain grasses and legumes appear in paddocks where we've never put seed.

As fall approaches we will need to set aside a certain number of paddocks for winter feed. This means some of the paddocks must be taken out of the fall rotation and be allowed to stockpile for the winter. Again, we will not set aside the same paddocks each fall. We use different winter paddocks in order to allow different areas of the ranch to reseed and mature. However, the low-lying paddocks must be avoided during wet periods of the year to minimize pugging. I like saving the upper and generally rockier paddocks for the mushy, wet times of the year. There is a real benefit in having a 20-acre paddock on a hilltop saved back when we get those 6-inch rains in November or mid-March. Three hundred cows and calves can do a great deal of damage to a pasture down in the bottomland when it has rained so much the creek is 6 feet above its bank.

As our system develops, we also realize that more paddocks are being allowed to grow to a higher point in the fall and before the growing season ends. This gives a larger and larger number of paddocks each year all with more inches in height of forage at the end of the growing season. Our total so-called *reserved forage* going into the winter becomes increased significantly over time. The actual practice of stockpiling can almost become a moot point. Because we have so many paddocks with taller residuals our total forage availability surpasses the need to reserve forage under the traditional stockpiling system. This is when adding more livestock could be beneficial.

This stockpiling of fall regrowth for winter forage can be viewed as contradictory to what we have learned about forage as it progresses through the stages of the growing cycle. If we set aside a certain amount of paddocks for stockpiling, we would have reduced the number of paddocks in our rotation. The impact is that we have shortened our factor of time allotted for rest in all the other paddocks. The cause of lack of forage is always due less to the stays in each paddock and has more to do with the inadequate amount of rest, or regrowth time, in all the paddocks. We have proven that once a forage obtains a height beyond Stage 2, its growth slows.

There is a critical balance between having adequate amounts of rapid growth in the majority of our paddocks while setting aside only the necessary stockpiled paddocks for winter forage. We should never sacrifice rapid forage growth in the bulk of our paddocks due to inadequate rest time in order to stockpile a few paddocks for winter feed. I prefer to have most of my paddocks at a height of 6 to 8 inches high than just a few at a 12-inch height. I do not want any paddocks at a very low height as we head into winter. Too many times a new grazier will be disappointed with his results from winter stockpiling for this reason. Reducing our overall forage production in order to stockpile a few paddocks is little different than mechanically harvesting in the fall so that we can have what seems to be large quantities of feed for the winter. This holds true for a drought situation as well. It always serves us better to save time rather than feed for the non-growth or slow-growth periods. Without exception we must always promote the maximum growth of all forage across the ranch.

If we plan our annual program of forage utilization to extend at least one month beyond the expected time for new growth to begin in the spring, our chances of having plenty of winter feed will be greatly increased.

This winter stockpile of forage is generally treated a little differently than the rotation during the rest of the year. For most of the year we have been moving the herd into a new paddock and shutting the gate behind them. This is so they are not allowed to walk and eat back over the forage they just came from. For our winter stockpile, and during our nongrowing period, we are going to strip graze each large paddock using polywire and step-in posts. Because winter is a time when most grasses become dormant, we are not concerned with cattle walking back over what they grazed on the day before.

Since we are only giving them each day what they will consume that day behind the polywire, we don't care if they back up. We may have only one water source in a 20-acre paddock. By stretching a polywire across the paddock and moving it forward only 20 to 100 feet at a time — depending upon the size of the paddock, amount of forage and number of cattle in the herd — the cattle can return to the single water source as we migrate our wire across the paddock. If we were to turn the herd into the entire 20 acres at once, most of the forage would be wasted before it could be eaten.

This type of grazing can improve our grazing efficiency from about 20% to well over 80%. It compares closely to what would happen if you put out 50 square bales of hay in the center of the pasture during the winter and turned in 100 cows. The cows would step on over half of the hay, and smash it into the mud and urinate and poop on most of the other half.

This strip grazing system works better with fescue pastures than any other forage. This doesn't mean that if you can't grow fescue you cannot strip graze during the winter. I strip graze many types of clovers and other grasses as well. It's just that long-stem fescue actually improves in value as the winter proceeds, and nothing holds up under extreme weather conditions like Kentucky 31 fescue.

I have found in some situations that stockpiling forages for winter feeding may not be the most aggressive management available. Some areas of the country do not grow forages that stockpile as well as fescue does. Some ranches — even in the fescue belt — have other species of grasses in abundance. We also must look at the growth curve of forages discussed earlier. In order to stockpile a great deal of grass for winter use, we must have allowed some of the forage to get to a height of above that 6- to 8-inch height. This is the height when the growth of most grasses will slow. Simple reasoning shows that if those pastures which were set aside for tall grass growth for winter feed were grazed while in that quick-growback stage below 6 inches, our total forage production would have been bigger. We would have been able to keep those pastures in the general rotation and had longer resting periods among all pastures, which would have produced more total forage. In other words, we may have been able to produce a larger total amount of forage by not stockpiling grasses for winter feed and running more cattle on the same ground.

If no stockpiling is to take place we must have an alternative system for winter feeding. I have found it sometimes economical in these instances to purchase what winter feed I required in the form of round bales of dairy-quality alfalfa and portion out the required amounts daily throughout the winter with a hay unroller on the bed of my farm truck. Again this is not possible for the startup rancher because his minimal investments in cattle and land do not include the luxury of a bale unroller. I believe this level of management can improve gross margin when used cautiously. The overproduction of grasses in the Midwest, typically substantial in the spring and less so in the fall, can be mechanically harvested by custom contractors with the carrying capacity of the ranch increased as well. The choice sometimes made to produce additional pounds of beef to sell because of the unevenness of forage growth throughout the year — due to varying amounts of rainfall and temperature changes — can have negative effects on gross margin. The increased management of mechanically harvested and mechanically fed forage might not prove to be economically beneficial, even under the control of seasoned ranchers. The efficiency goal of trying to utilize every single blade of grass to its upmost can be as treacherous as trying to wean off the biggest calf in the county when it comes down to net profits.

8
Soil to Man

A COW CAN BE ONE OF THE MOST DESTRUCTIVE CREATURES on the ranch if confined by man and restricted from doing what she does best. Allowed to perform at optimum, she will only take from the earth what she needs to procreate and ensure her species survives. In leaving behind her excrements and sharp hoof actions, under natural conditions she will only improve the forage production of the soil. Our mismanagement practices of monoculture pastures, heavy application of chemical pesticides, and indiscriminate salt fertilizer use deter not only the economic productiveness of the bovine, but these practices can severely reduce available nutrient levels in the soil.

The cow, being an expert nutritionist and chemist, will seek out the available nutrition from a variety of grasses, legumes, forbs, herbs and woody species to meet her needs. A clean fencerow, resembling the edges of a golf course, can be a nutritional barrier for the cow. Fencerows or designated strips should be full of wild herbs, brush and forbs that make up the medicine cabinet for the cow. Our farms and ranches are much more than some rich man's pastime in which he manicures his pastures like a city estate. This mismanagement of forage land into prizes of man's ego is a thief among all of us in broad daylight.

Foraging land is a limited resource of grand value. That value is the worth we place on human life. It is a selfish endeavor to manage forage land in any way that it will not produce quality food. An ill-advised landowner is inadvertently raising the price of all food by not educating himself and then practicing good forage production. With the economic laws of supply and demand, when a producer limits valuable production he limits supply to some of those who may be marginal buyers, even at highly efficient production. If this poor-quality producer shrinks supply, he may be raising the level at which some buyers may be able to purchase food for the family.

We can observe the cow to gain a better understanding of how efficient she is at searching a pasture for the specific nutrients she requires. When this chemist finds her way out of the monoculture pasture and chooses to browse through the briars and variety of cockleburs, chickweed and wild chicory growing along the roadside or in the hedgerow, she is seeking to improve her own nutrition, nutrition we have ignorantly deprived her. Our reaction is generally one of anger at the cow for pushing her way through the boundaries which we have constrained her. We must spend time observing her actions and learn from what she is trying to tell us. She says, but only if we listen, that she does not want or need that expensive supplement from the bag purchased from the feedstore to meet her nutritional requirements. Simply allow some of the fencerow, on her side of the fence, to mature and bring forth from deep in the soil nutrients which are lacking in the shallow-rooted plants we force her to eat in so-called improved pastures.

Soon we will recognize that by initiating a soil-to-cow forage program the cow-chemist's reproductive ability increasingly becomes the shortest route to improved economics on our ranch. By simply allowing a larger variety of mostly so-called weeds to grow and become available nutrition to the cow, the droppings she leaves behind nourishes the soil by way of biological activity. This below-the-surface increase in microbes, earthworms, etc., — and in dung beetles — increases the organic matter, building sufficient humus, which in turn produces a more nutrient-dense sward of forage. The milk and meat produced from this improved swath of forages also contains improved levels of nutrients. Ultimately mankind has the most to gain from this soil-to-man chain of events.

When the meat- and milk-producing cow is limited to only a few species and varieties of forage her nutrient intake will be compromised. This limited intake will in turn reduce the quality of food we receive when we consume that meat and milk. This is not a nutrient-dense food product. Our obligation as ranchers and farmers is to provide the most nutrient-dense foods we are capable of producing at fair market values. It is no grand gesture to produce and distribute thousands of acres of a so-called food to large numbers of people if we are causing them damage. As Americans we have seen a shortage of production in nutrient-dense foods. Even something as simple as the protein content in field corn has dropped to below 6.5%. In years past a farmer took pride in his corn production when his crop tested over 12% protein, the measurement of bushels or pounds of production per acre only having meaning if the bushels and pounds were nutrient-dense. Awards and empty recognition are given to farmers and producers who have mastered high production. This high production is slow death to the small child who is starving for required minerals now deficient in this award-winning crop. It is a tragedy to die of starvation with a full stomach.

What are the steps that I take to turn around such a worn-out soil and make it productive once again? What I do not do is go to town and purchase chemical fertility, even in the form of calcium from limestone, which is the general practice in my area. The deep-rooted chicory plant will bring up calcium from 12 to 18 feet below and store it in its 4- to 6-foot stalks over the summer. When the cows are turned into this paddock with standing forage — where the cattle have been kept out for over 100 days — they stomp down these very mature stalks. Within these stalks reside many nutrients, including calcium. The hooves of the cows lay these chicory stalks down to the ground where the livestock beneath the soil surface can begin their job. They first pull this carbon down and begin building soil organic matter which perpetuates itself into more and more biological activities, including increases in both quantity and diversity of micro-organisms. This laying down of the rich calcium once hidden deep below the soil surface becomes more available to short-rooted plants once deprived of calcium and other elements now made available from acids breaking down the stores from the systems of organic matter and humus.

Worn-out soil may show little chance for improvement in the beginning stages. One's first thoughts are to go on the market and purchase the missing elements in order to bring up the shortages shown on the soil test results. These are old-school teachings that have very little, if any, value on the livestock ranch. These chemical additives, like anhydrous ammonia or potassium chloride, only work at destroying biological activity in the soil.

Another practice would be to spray herbicides to help destroy the undesirable woody species and the class of mostly unknown plants most people refer to as weeds. These so-called weeds like lamb's-quarter, pigweed, plantain, burnet, chicory and many, many other varieties and species of forbs and herbs — are more nutritious to the livestock and the soil than many of the so-called domesticated grasses sold at outrageous prices at the seed supply store. In most cases all the seed we need on our farms is already in the soil bank. Stored there for generations are millions of dormant seeds. Some seeds were placed there by previous operators of the farm; many others blew in on the wind, or were carried on wings and hooves over many years by creatures both large and small. Why would I spend money on domesticated seeds when free, higher-quality seeds will bring forth forages that will grow my livestock? My only job is to disturb the soil with the hooves of the cattle so that the dormant seeds will have an opportunity to express themselves and go to work on my ranch. These plants then will be feed for my livestock. They will provide nutrition for the species both above and below the ground. What the cow does not eat, she stomps into the ground for an increase in organic matter.

No matter how sparse the forages are, the need to keep the livestock moving from paddock to paddock never ceases. Even during the winter months manure and urine needs to be spread evenly among all paddocks. When forages are no longer adequate for nutrition for the livestock, the supplementation with stored forages like hay or silage begins. And until spring brings new grass, the cattle and other livestock continue to be moved through the rotation. Manure should never be allowed to pile up in one area and its valuable nutrients be wasted.

In the early stages of improving old, worn-out pastures, shortages of forage will occur early in the year on a well-stocked farm or ranch, as well as the expected winter shortages. As each successive winter goes by and the system of holistic planned grazing is practiced, the need for winter supplementation is extended later into the season until one year, hay feeding is almost eliminated or started only just before spring arrives. This is the time to consider adding more livestock to the operation. As the practice of building soil organic matter creates more biology in the soil, more and more forages will begin to take the place of undesirable woody species and cover bare spots on the ground. Many paddocks that may have only been capable of producing 1,200 or 1,400 lbs. of dry matter to the acre are now producing 3,000 or 4,000 lbs. to the acre annually. This increase of carrying capacity is the result of soil restoration through persistent rotation of the cow herd throughout the ranch with long rest periods of over 90 days between grazings. The soil organic matter will increase providing humus with the necessary acids to break down mineral substances and release more available plant nutrients.

The sequestering of elements, like nitrogen, both from the soil and the atmosphere builds on the idea of creating more forage for the addition of even more livestock to the farm or ranch. All this and even more production can occur when we make the final decision to remove all substances ending in the suffix -*icides* — herbicides, pesticides, etc., — from our standard farming practices of livestock and forage production. If the cow we have cannot be productive without the additive of annual chemical treatments for both external or internal parasites, the consideration should be in the forefront that this animal may need to find a new home. She can then be replaced by one that can exist in a more sustainable manner.

9

Time to Think

I HAVE MANY FRIENDS AND ACQUAINTANCES all across this great country. Many are farmers and ranchers, yet many are working people raising their families in the city or small towns. There are also many who own small acreages in the country and commute to their place of employment, generally in a non-agricultural field. Wherever these people live and work, most all of them have the same complaint. The gripe that I hear most often goes something like this, "I have been so busy lately I don't know if I'm coming or going. The Mrs. and I both work too many hours each day. We never have a sit down meal together other than the holidays. Our kids play ball three nights a week and practice the other four. I'm lucky if I get to bed before 11 or 12 o'clock, then it's up at 5 a.m. to start all over." Most of the farm and ranch people have the same problem, but they add, "I use my vacation time to put up hay, my weekends working cattle,

I work all the overtime at work I can just to keep the farm above water. We never have time for anything."

Because I myself once lived a life like my friends above are living now, I know precisely what they are talking about. We have been taught at an early age to be either passive to the extreme or frantically busy to avoid having any so-called wasted time. With very few exceptions, our early training seldom involved the necessity for time management. This time management I am referring to has nothing to do with an attempt to get as much work done each day as humanly possible. It has a great deal to do with managing your affairs in a manner which provides you with time for reflection and thought for good decision making. How valid is the argument if it was our decision to work 12 hours a day to make top money, if after 10 years or so our marriages fall apart, our children become distant relatives, and instead of actually building wealth we generally build excessive debt in stuff of little value. High earnings have brought very little happiness to most people in the long run.

I have owned a few new vehicles in my life. That smell of a new pickup truck really brings a person joy — for a flash in time. Then, after a while, after a few dents and dings, a few too narrow gate openings, and a bull or two, it drives and feels pretty much like any other farm truck I ever owned. This attitude of having an overabundance of "stuff" is simply not worth the trouble. There is no justification in the end. This life we live is not on a trial basis. This is the only one we get. The ridiculously busy lifestyle that many have given in to is not healthy for our bodies, families, souls, relationships, and certainly can be devastating to our cow operation. This fast-paced type of lifestyle is not sustainable.

A cow/calf ranch does not require 12-hour days to be financially rewarding. In fact, I have proposed before that in our current times, 2010, a family can make a comfortable living with about a 300-cow herd even with moderate debt selling commodity beef. This size cow herd can be managed by a husband and wife team quite efficiently with a very small work schedule on the ranch for both. The difficulty arises when the "wants" outdo the "needs" on an unbalanced scale. Another term we could use is *greed*. A wise fellow once told me a silly little phrase that has stayed with me these many years. He said, "Little pigs are cute, but hogs get butchered." I believe that even for city dwellers with no desire to farm, this could apply.

To run a business, in this case a cow/calf ranch, at a supersonic pace from morning until night, day after day, year after year, is a certain recipe for disaster. Man has definite limitations and as individuals our successes will increase when we become better at acknowledging our own limitations. We cannot spend every day working the operation from a physical and mechanical perspective and avoid the pitfalls that are destined to meet us almost daily. There must be ample time each day for reflection on the husbandry of the cattle operation. In our case the need may not be to stop and smell the roses, but to stop and smell the forage. If a person spends 12 hours in a day on the tractor, his concern about biological activity in the soil is probably going to be the last thing on his mind, if considered at all. A pasture walk — not ride — of every paddock on the ranch should be done at least once a week. This does not mean that a scheduled two-hour period is planned every Tuesday for a rushed inspection of the ranch. Some part of a pasture walk should be accomplished almost daily in one paddock or more. It should be a time of reflection on and observation of all that can be seen. A binder of some kind for note taking should be brought along. The walk might take only 30 minutes some days, and other days it might take four hours.

We have to take time to observe what the cows are eating and how they move from one area to the next. Are they spending time along the fencerows seeking forage not available to them in the pastures? Are some of the fences holding up better than others because of differences in construction? If we take time to dig around in the manure piles, are we finding ample numbers of dung beetles? This could be a reflection of our mineral cycling. Do the pastures show signs of bare areas, places where certain grasses are too thin? These are the fundamentals of community dynamics.

This time wandering the ranch is an enjoyable time for me personally. I love being out with the cattle, in the pastures, the woods, digging around poop, checking stands of grass, observing cattle behaviors, watching how all things on the ranch are so connected to each other. This connectedness is the basis for holistic management. Each and every move or change we make on the ranch is related in some shape or form to another aspect of the ranch. No decision made is made in isolation. The realization soon comes that any single change I make on my ranch can and will have an effect on something else on the ranch. If my time is so limited that I can't find the time to compare and analyze these effects, I will surely make disastrous mistakes one after another.

Spending a great deal of time simply observing is critical to the success of biological farming and ranching. A seemingly simple notion that the numbers of insect-eating birds are appearing to decline on the ranch will be unnoticed by a workaholic. For example, maybe the birds no longer have a proper place to nest, or their food supply is diminished because I cleaned all the fencerows out and left no suitable habitat. And now grasshoppers are destroying what little pasture I have during the dry summer times, because the birds are no longer around in large enough numbers to keep the grasshoppers under control. These observations, and an unlimited number of others, will seldom be seen during a rushed 12-hour workday. We can take time to manage better if we take the time to see what is really going on at the ranch down at the ground level. It is this ground level that the cows are working from.

As our employees, these cows can tell us in many, many different ways how to be more efficient with our operations. A sure sign that something is going wrong is when we are rushing around just to get the necessities accomplished each day — the mundane, common chores. Our plates can be too full and yet we still are not getting anywhere. An effort must be made to not allow ourselves to fill all of the hours of the day with tasks to do. The unexpected should be expected. By filling our workday like a dispatcher fills a calendar we are not allowing for the accidents and unplanned problems that are certain to come our way. Not only does planning get pushed to the side by demanding such a great amount from our physical bodies, but when the unplanned happens late in the evening we tend to take out the problems on those around us. This will escalate into disaster if it happens too many times a week. We can build space within our schedule to better handle most of what the ranch and life throws our way when we can get a handle on our greed and the senseless need to keep busy for every hour we are not sleeping.

Time spent planning is the answer for many of the problems that arise on the ranch throughout the year. As these minor occurrences make themselves visible, our first thoughts will be that the root of the problem is external. We will blame the low cattle market, high cost of hay, daylight savings time, or whatever seems appropriate and available at the time. If we were able, and most are not, to stand back and look at what it was or what series of events that took place to get us in the predicament we are currently in this time, we could see that if the proper planning had been accomplished at an earlier date we would have been prepared for these circumstances. Notice that I did not say that all the problems would be solved. Difficulties will still arise. However, with planning we can foresee a great deal of these situations in advance and have a plan of action to minimize their effects and to deal with the variables.

I am going to attempt to explain a sequence of planning that should take place to help avoid disaster. Remember, planning alone is not going to guarantee success. It will not even make everything flow smoothly. Planning excels in the area of giving you alternatives for many of the possible *what ifs* as they come along. And be assured many challenges will come along no matter how positive your outlook or how well-bred your cow herd.

I will be the first to admit that this late in the book does not seem to be the time to begin the planning stages for your livestock enterprise. But just like the discussion of accounting principles for your farm, if I would have started this book with a detailed study of accelerated depreciation or creating holistic goals, many of you would not have read this far. I am a stockman and a forage nut at heart. My interest, just like most all other farmers and ranchers, is much higher if I hear the speaker mention the words *cow* or *white clover*. Very few of us cowboy types will spare even 10 minutes to read up on the management of our livestock operations, unless we are forced to. This "force" generally comes during or after failure. I am certain many failing ranches could have been saved had planning been put in its proper place of priority. Not unlike most, I would much rather attend a bull sale than a business seminar. But isn't *business* what we are really doing? Many of us can spot a poor-performing cow, a bad spot in the fence, or even a declining pasture, but we fail to see that it will be our own poor planning that takes much of what we value highly away from us. And yes, this book should have begun with a chapter on creating your holistic goals. So now that you are into this book this far, you might as well hang in for the duration.

In the book *Holistic Management*, Allan Savory very simply states that your holistic goals start with stating the *quality of life, forms of production* and *future resource base*. This planning stage should begin before the first cow has been purchased. But even if you have been able to hang on ranching for 20 or more years, it will never be too late to start this process. This is an investment in your business, just the same as raising or acquiring a herd sire. In fact, I dare say without this planning stage and implementation of its dimensions, the best pedigrees and your ranching success will fade as quickly as the denim in your new Wranglers.

Once these three areas have been thoroughly planned, one can refer to them individually and determine whether or not a future action is sustainable by subjecting it to a test to see if it meets planned requirements. The sustainability test is the "test all" for each action to be considered in the future. Sustainability extends much further than simple profitability. It may be profitable for me to lease the 1,000-acre ranch 80 miles down the road to run a group of mama cows on, but if because of this new responsibility my time is so severely divided that my family falls apart, then this venture is not sustainable after all. After these three facets have been clearly identified it will become much clearer to everyone involved in the operation if an action should be taken or not.

The quality of life you are seeking will be the first of the holistic goals to consider. In my case, it is imperative to me and my family that we maintain a lifestyle that keeps us together at the ranch for the greatest part of each day as possible. For example, if a new venture requires me or my wife to be gone two or three overnight stays each week, then that project would fail our quality-of-life test.

We know our quality of life will eventually suffer if I take on a project or a job in which I am continually away from the ranch for long periods of time. In essence, we can look at it a different way. Once quality of life has been defined, we can look at all activities as if they fit into the category of what I want to do or things I don't want to do. If I find myself involved in many activities I simply do not want to do on a regular basis, I and the people around me are going to be very unhappy. This is clearly not sustainability, which has no correlation to profits at all. Many of us get into a problem in this area when money is involved. If we place making money as the guiding priority in our lives, then all else — including quality of life — takes a backseat. For an activity or action to be sustainable it must be within the guidelines of our quality-of-life statement.

When viewing our forms of production we sometimes see only the somewhat narrow focus of our current operation. We may say that our only form of production is commodity beef in our cow/calf operation. This dismisses the possibility of hunting leases during deer season, a corn maze in the fall, and many other choice methods to earn income from the same land base. We must be careful not to smash imagination and also to lose flexibility in our ability to earn revenue from our land businesses. However, we also must be careful not to chase every possibility that crosses our minds. Subjecting our choices to the other tests in this process can help eliminate many poor choices.

When evaluating how your decisions affect your future resource base, we are generally talking about land if you are a rancher like me. Understocking the ranch in order to finance some alternative venture may cause such a decrease in stocking rates that the stands of forage will begin to decrease; this is known as community dynamics. This, in turn, may decrease mineral cycling and the quality as well as the quantity of forage. Therefore the total landscape of the ranch could take on a different look than what your stated future resource base was intended. Although there are many variables to analyze when making decisions on a ranch, these three topics, which help make up your holistic goals, should be referred to often and with clarity.

I believe that this approach to holistic management and putting these three action-based queries into writing is comparable to what a large corporation attempts when it writes its mission statement. In many instances a mission statement could be helpful in the decision-making process when operating a ranch. But stating some of the attributes that make up the mission statement in a more detailed form, as described above, allows those involved to better grasp the choices available over and over during the life of a ranch. Having this guide will help keep us on the road to where we want to go while minimizing unnecessary detours along the way.

10
Local Adaptation

FOR YEARS I EXERCISED THE PRACTICE OF LOADING UP A GROUP OF COWS and their calves into a stock trailer and moved them to another farm I had rented for when the grass became too scarce on the farm they were on. Sometimes I would move the entire herd, and other times I might move only a substantial percentage of the herd. I thought at the time this move was mandated due to shortage of rainfall, a late spring, or some other phenomenon out of my control. Looking back, with a clearer point of view that experience and distance from the problem sometimes provides, I see things quite differently. The scarcity of forage that the cattle were having was primarily due to my mismanagement of the cattle and grass operation as a functioning organism. The available grass on my farms has always been more subject to my daily management than regular rainfall. By allowing a group of cattle to roam at will over large-sized pastures or entire farms was the onset of certain forage shortage downtrack. Stock density and stocking rates are subjects covered better in other chapters. But it is this poor management of cattle numbers on paddock size that eventually led me to other misfortunes.

When these cattle were relocated to another farm — sometimes just 10 miles down the road and other times to a neighboring county — the move would always be followed by a slump in livestock performance in that herd. As in the case of the cow herself, calving problems and breed-back were generally the first financial results that got my attention. The poor performance of the cattle, lower rates of gain and a fall in the overall condition to a lower level, would many times be unobserved during my hectic schedule of always using my back more often than good sense. Foot problems would increase and culling rates for many other abnormalities would follow. The learned practice of substituting machinery, animal science, and general ignorance of good animal husbandry was taking my herd in a downward spiral almost without my noticing. And my misjudgments and bad decisions would have led to ruination if not corrected by accepting the notion of local adaptation. I now have discovered that the cow again is much more than a mowing machine. She is the most important part of a farming organism which survives above the ground while the soil biology is below the ground. Just as the change that occurs to the biological activity in the soil will certainly affect the forages produced on that farm, a change in diet for the cow from farm to farm will have an effect on her abilities as she performs her part in this larger organism we call the farm enterprise. The cow had adapted to the farm she was on before the move. It was not that one farm is any more or less superior to the other, but the cow had grown accustomed to the forage quality of the first farm.

Our modern way of agriculture does not take into consideration the importance of local adaptation. We have been taught that machinery and science can replace good animal husbandry. Since the college class once called "animal husbandry" has now been changed to "animal science," we have at least a full generation of farmers whose understanding of animal husbandry mainly includes injecting something from a syringe or supplementing from a purchased bag. The idea that cows and soil should not be transportable or disposable and that each are vital elements in the larger organism of farming is mostly ignored. The welfare of the cow, the farm, and civilization as a whole depends on man's willingness to accept the responsibility passed along when he received this higher level of intelligence than any other creature. The master workings of a farm involve science not because we have gained the ability to identify some of the elements of soil biology. The science of this organism has been present since the beginning of time. When we get in the way and ignore good animal husbandry practices such as "local adaptation," we are taking a step backward in science.

As the soil erosion due to monoculture farming continues to eat away at our future ability to produce, devastatingly harsh salt fertilizers, dangerous chemical pesticides, herbicides and fungicides, GMO foods, and the prostitution of seeds so they will not reproduce, our good use of husbandry will become even more important to humanity should we choose not to starve to death.

A positive attitude coupled with action in the form of managed grazing will turn the biological and economical tables for the livestock producer. There has been no other recognized invention, practice, or whiz-bang gizmo of any kind that has gotten me more excited about the future of ranching. A well-thought-out system of multi-species grazing on multiple species and wide varieties of plants under a planned grazing system with proper genetics can return profitability and happiness to the farm and ranch.

It was the adaptation of the cow to the first farm that allowed her to perform better than when I moved her to the new farm. She not only had grown accustomed to the forages at the first farm, but the water, favorite shade trees, the sounds she would hear from the creek, and the distant familiar voices she would wake up to each day. That first farm was her home. I have learned that cows are much more than personal property. They are not thoughtless, simplistic machines. When I loaded that group of cows up and moved them to another farm the stress that was brought to that family of cows is much greater than the human mind can conceive. I can verify this by the tremendous increase in open cows the next year within this herd. Weaning weights will decline and the overall poor condition of the cows will lead me to no other conclusion.

We know that few events forced upon a human family other than a move to a new home in a new city causes greater stress on a household. And unlike the children in a home, we are not able to sit down with the cow herd and discuss the many important reasons for the move. Such moves should be avoided at almost any cost. Management should be implemented which does not require the regular- or irregular-transport of a herd from farm to farm.

The purchase of a new bull or heifer from a distant herd can cause the same calamities when we make these additions to the cow herd. My own mistakes, which I repeated many times over many years without realizing the total costs of my actions, in purchasing so-called quality bulls from the most current and popular bloodlines across the country brought about adaptation problems. The common practice that most seedstock producers have to this day of developing their bulls on high-protein and/or high-energy rations from a bag leads to huge problems for the cowman.

As cow/calf producers we have now learned that to be profitable the cattle on our ranch must be able to perform on what the ranch can produce. We cannot afford the extravagances of grain and other high-cost inputs here on the ranch. The cow is a foraging animal and foraging is what she must do well. The bulls that we purchase to place into our herd must have been raised in similar conditions as our cow herd if adaptation problems are going to be minimized. Of course, the words that I have written in preceding chapters discuss the absolute necessity of raising our own bulls and replacement heifers. But just like many cowmen in our country still do today, for over 25 years I also purchased all of my bulls from other seedstock producers with the intention of improving my herd through heifer retention from those bulls on my cows. The result was that most of those grain-developed bulls would fall apart within the first year or two on my grass-based cattle ranch. I found more than once I would need to purchase three bulls to do the work one good bull should be capable of performing. These bulls could simply not adapt to their new home.

Livestock tend to be able to adjust to changes well if the changes are gradual and to their liking. How do we know if a cow likes something or not? She will lose weight, not rebreed, or perhaps even die if we force too many changes on her at one time. One way to put this concept into very plain terms is that when it really comes down to it the cow is just not very adaptable. This very large, living, breathing, caring animal puts great importance on the smallest, most seemingly insignificant changes. It may not even be important to understand if these changes are actually nutritional differences from one farm or ranch to the next, or more personal. Maybe she is simply extremely sensitive. Either way, she is not going to adapt well at all to moves. This resistance to adapting to a new environment is costly to the producer. This is a cost that we simply cannot accept. Our management must reflect this.

11
Multi-Species Grazing

EVER SINCE I WAS A SMALL BOY I DREAMED of being a cattle rancher. I thought the stories I read about the fights between the sheepherders and the cowboys were learning experiences in allowable discrimination. Nowhere did I ever read as a child, or even as an adult until just a few years ago, that the idea of running cows and sheep together had some real economic advantages. The sheep guys had their reasons for raising sheep, the cowmen had their reasons for raising cattle, and they did not seem to care for each other. What a fool I have been.

I now have about 150 head of hair sheep running with my cow herd, which is quickly growing to about 500 pair. I intend on doubling my sheep herd over the next few years, and maybe even more if things keep going like they have been recently. The sheep are to a certain extent browsers, and cattle are grazers. What does this mean? Sheep will tend to eat many of the more woody species of plants that the cow generally reserves for last choice. The cow is a dead-end host for sheep parasites, and it works the other way around as well. The sheep and cow act as a companion crop of livestock when managed together on the same ranch. Since I have been an open-minded sheep rancher along with my cattle for some time now, I am happy to report that I must have received wrong information years ago and have been carrying a misguided grudge against sheep. Several large sheep and cattle ranchers I have met out west have happily informed me that during the many times the price of cattle fell below acceptable levels if it hadn't been for their sheep they would have lost their ranches. The story is now clear that it wasn't the cow that settled the Wild West, it was the sheep herds.

The hair sheep that I raise on my ranch with the cattle have been the most trouble-free females I have ever known. Unlike the cow, the ewe can easily have three birthings every two years. And if that is not enough, she generally has twins and sometimes triplets. And here is the real benefit: her offspring will butcher and the females will breed and go into the herd the same year they are born. Compare this to the production of a cow and we should wonder why we are not all raising sheep. The market price for lamb is quite comparable to weaned calves, so there is no problem on the marketing end of things either.

The main problem I hear from first-time sheep herders is their problems with parasites. I tend to blame this on two primary problems. One is in the selection of the seedstock, and the other is the management of forages.

A good set of ewes can produce on what the ranch produces. You have read this before in these pages concerning cattle. It is the same with the sheep. Acquire a healthy set of ewes and close the gate. Quit buying new problems and opening the ranch up to anything that has a potential to deteriorate the quality of the herd. The sheep that will improve your herd are generally already on your ranch. Use the same selection techniques for sheep as for cattle. Some of the new ewes will perform and some will have to be taken from the herd. Selection will become extremely important to the productivity of the sheep herd. One of the positive things I have found with the work I've done on my sheep herd is that success comes much faster than with the cow herd simply because of their fast rate of growth and shorter gestation period, as well as their ability to twin regularly.

The second part of the equation concerning sheep problems is their susceptibility to parasites. This is a real situation, but it is quite manageable. In a well-managed holistic system of planned grazing the sheep are moved around the ranch just as with cattle. With long rest periods for the paddocks, along with the grazing effects of the cattle, the paddocks become less infested with parasites which will give problems to the sheep once they graze again. I have found that a 90-day rest period for each paddock after grazing with the sheep all but eliminates the problems of parasites in my sheep. In the rare occasion that a ewe cannot function under these conditions on my ranch, she simply must find a new home immediately. The addition of sheep to my cattle ranch has offered nothing but opportunities for increases in profit.

Although I have been truly satisfied with the addition of sheep to my cattle ranch, sheep were not the first species I added. We have had a family milk cow for many years. My good wife has been completely in charge of that area of the ranch and is still today. This is not some sexist issue; my wife simply likes Jersey milk cows in general. The simple task of having a single family Jersey milk cow for our own household milk, cream and butter eventually grew to about six cows in total. My wife now supplies raw Jersey milk to many other families each week. She milks her cows with a bucket milker in an old six-stanchion barn next to our house once a day. Her holistic system of no-grain, grass-fed dairying involves allowing each cow to raise her own calf while also providing one to two additional gallons of milk for sale each day. She calls her cows into a new paddock in the evenings, and leaves the calves in the previous pasture overnight separated from their mothers. After she milks the cows in the morning, she simply turns the cows back out with their babies and repeats this again in the evening. With the good price we receive for raw

Jersey cow milk and the terrific demand for the product, we are very happy with this system.

A small herd of Jersey milk cows is an almost essential ingredient to any sustainable farm or ranch. The increase in income by adding a milk cow or two, or three or more, is well worth the adjustment. It must be recognized that the difficulty in locating the right kind of dairy cow — one that will perform on what the ranch produces — is just as much a challenge as finding beef cows or sheep. Generally speaking, they cannot be bought. They must be raised for all the same reasons discussed concerning the beef cows early in these chapters about adaptation. Through many years of trial and error it is now clear that no matter what animal is brought onto the ranch the concepts of adaptation and the correct phenotype for grass remain the same.

Another challenge with the business of selling raw milk to customers is supply and demand, or the challenge of matching the exact amount of milk supply your customers demand each day. At certain times you will be squeezing every drop from every cow to fill the day's orders. Then in a couple of days you might have surplus volume to contend with. This is where the pig enterprise becomes helpful.

We now raise a small herd of foraging hogs on the ranch. There are very few things a healthy pig will not eat. They don't like onions or orange peels, but they will do anything for the leftover milk from the dairy barn. We now have three sows and a boar that supply all of our pork customers with the most sumptuous acorn-finished pork anywhere. We raise our hogs in small two wire paddocks. Each paddock of about five acres has a mixture of mostly oak timber with matches of quality forage. And yes, pigs love clover, pigweed, chicory and many of the other forages that our cows and sheep eat as well. Once your customer tastes a porkchop from a grass- and acorn-grazing hog, they realize what has been masqueraded as pork from pigs raised in crates and only fed GMO corn is not worth taking home. And any of the leftover milk can easily go to the hogs as it only adds to the flavor and quality of the meat. Of course, you must decide who gets the milk each day, because there is another species of farm animals that make up an important part of the ranch. Chickens will also do anything for a pail of raw milk.

Our chickens are divided between two demographics. You can either be a laying hen with a long life of maybe eight or nine years or longer, or you can be a broiler with a lifespan of about six to eight weeks. We run about 250 laying hens in a portable henhouse pulled across the pastures. These hens supply all the eggs we currently have customers for and then some. But no egg ever goes to waste on this ranch. Any leftover eggs are fed to the eat-everything-in-sight porkers in the woods. When the grass is growing and plentiful these egg layers get very little food in the form of feed from a bag. And when these girls are not laying eggs they are fertilizing the paddocks. The holistic system I describe takes all these component enterprises and puts them to work for the common good of the ranch and the rancher's family. It is not by chance or luck that one species either feeds or promotes the health of the other. This is accomplished by design.

The other chickens on this ranch are known as the broilers or fryers. They live a very happy outdoor life. It's just that they get all of their happiness in about eight weeks or less. These birds are raised on pasture as well in portable pens called chicken tractors. We purchase chicks from a local hatchery and receive them by mail. After spending a short time under a heatlamp at night, they are moved to the chicken tractors and fed all they want in forage and a non-GMO chicken feed formulated for growth. The chicken tractors are moved twice a day so that the birds always have fresh, clean, healthy forage to eat. It is best to have a plan in place that will minimize the carrying of water and feed. And again, behind the droppings of the broilers will grow some of the best forage on the ranch.

I don't know how many different species a ranch can support. We add additional species to our ranch as we feel we have the capabilities to do a good job. I recently began stocking some of the ponds with catfish and will eventually offer filets from our freezers along with the other meats. My neighbor now raises quail along with her broilers. We are currently taking orders for the first turkeys we will sell to our customers. Each enterprise becomes more profitable as it feeds or promotes the growth of another. I became very interested in raising catfish when a fellow rancher told me how he fed the leftovers from processing to his catfish. His customers fight over who gets his limited supply of fresh fish.

These simple systems of production are far ahead of conventional agriculture and the quality of food produced is far beyond conventional and industrial ag systems. I find it almost humorous when I hear agribusiness experts make claims about their great efficiencies as an excuse for producing poor-quality foods. And I cringe when organic production is criticized as being food for the rich. I am now producing more pounds of food per acre and at a much higher quality than I ever did with my old system on mono- species cattle raising of big weaned calves supported with tons of inputs that only decreased efficiency and was leading me out of agriculture altogether. The holistic system of raising different species of livestock on a farm or ranch is real agriculture.

Photo Tour of the Rockin H Ranch

Cody, Dawnnell and Taylor Holmes' Rockin H Ranch is located near Norwood, Missouri, about 60 miles east of Springfield in the Ozarks. This region of the Ozarks, while beautiful, is known for thin, out-of-balance soils and poor agricultural production.

Rockin H Ranch

1,000 Acres
117+ Paddocks
Year-round Grazing

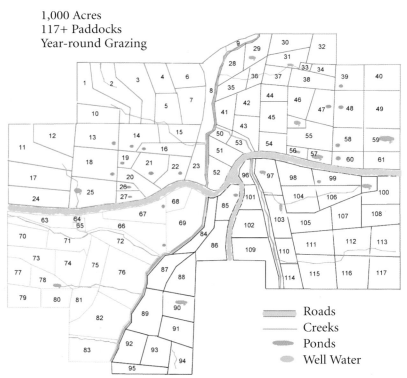

There are five different grazing cells, each with many individual paddocks. Each cell is approximately 200 acres; each paddock is about 5 acres.

This photo of a typical Ozark farm stands in stark contrast to the lush pastures found on Rockin H Ranch. Located in the same county, it lacks the forage density and diversity that is evident throughout Holmes' ranch.

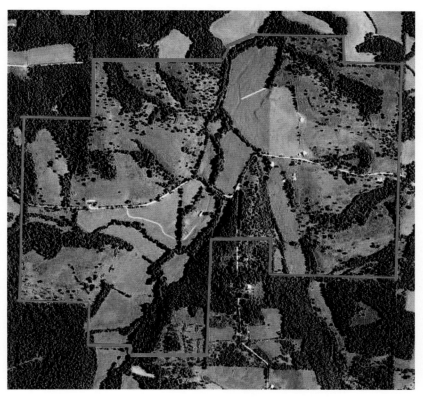

A desire to ranch runs deep. Cody and his siblings are seen with his pony, Shorty, and a homemade pony cart, circa 1968.

Dawnnell Hughes, future milkmaid, on her horse, Princess, with her brother in 1974.

Cowboy Cody, left in 1963. Pat Walton Holmes, right, and Cody's sister Patty. They grew up on a dairy farm and are bottle feeding calves here, photographed in 1970.

Both sides of the author's family, maternal and paternal, have only ever farmed as far back as traceable, at least six generations. This photo of his grandfather, John Mack Walton, was taken in the early 1940s.

The heart of the system centers on contented cows eating fresh, diverse, healthful forage.

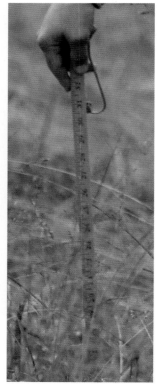

Forage is regularly measured on the ranch. Forage typically measures over 2 feet tall, right.

One of the benefits of Holistic Systems ranching: an 8-inch earthworm found on the ranch.

A dung beetle is seen in fresh cow manure.

Dense, waist-high, multi-species forages are seen throughout the ranch.

Not only is forage density high, but diversity is high as well. In a year's time livestock graze on almost 200 different species and varieties of plants.

Ragweed, as well as pigweed, is one of the two most nutritious plants on the farm, providing higher levels of almost every nutritional element than alfalfa.

The cattle are making their daily move across the road from the black grazing cell to the red grazing cell, as coded for management purposes (see the map on page 134).

The cattle are making one of their daily moves. Notice the cattle immediately start grazing through the gate.

The use of an ATV for the daily moving of cattle reduces management time on the ranch.

A pasture is seen before grazing.

Brown litter left over after grazing; something for the soil microbiology to consume.

Tall grass planned grazing is seen in action.

An Argentine-style gate — simply a 10' section of 4" PVC pipe with a slot cut at the end — lifts the high-tensile permanent wire fencing, creating a temporary gate wherever needed.

E. coli-free, clean bedding is always available for the livestock.

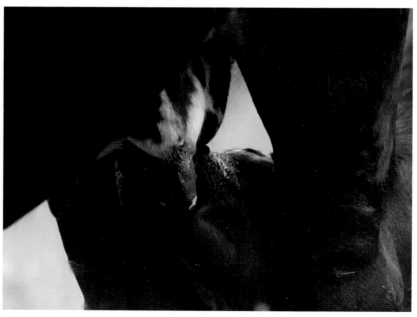

A calf is nursing from its mother.

Forages are often as tall as a cow's back.

Some animals even find nutrition in tree leaves above.

Planned mob grazing underway.

The herd at work on a paddock under the management of planned mob grazing.

A paddock after planned mob grazing.

Planned mob grazing of dense forages.

A pre-grazing grass density of 8,000 lbs. dry matter per acre is taken down by the herd to a post-grazing level of 1,000 lbs./acre. Polywire fencing is integral to the definition of paddocks on the ranch, as well as the daily moving of the cattle.

Cattle are strip grazing annual Sudan grass. This method utilizes the highest stock density for the shortest period of time; now commonly called mob grazing. Annuals were planted in the early stage of improving the farm. Now the farm is completely perennial plants.

Multi-species grazing at work on Rockin H Ranch: Emma, one of the Jersey cows, sheep and chickens can be seen in this single pasture.

Multi-species grazing of sheep and chickens.

Chickens are seen foraging on a pasture, usually following cattle by three to four days. The chickens eat fly larvae from the manure and serve as a form of biological fly control.

A mother hen teaches her chicks to forage for grass and insects.

This mobile chicken trailer provides nesting for the layers, protection from predators at night, and fresh grass and insects as needed.

A Production Red laying hen is seen inside the chicken trailer, one of several breeds of laying hens.

A pig forages for clover, above, while another pig forages through the snow.

A sow and pig foraging, right.

Taylor, daughter of Cody and Dawnnell Holmes, feeds her pig a mixture of forages, below.

Beef and pork do mix. Cattle and pigs are grazing together on a pasture without detriment to either.

Calves and piglets are seen grazing together. The pigs remain on a grazing cell longer than cattle. Another portable chicken house is seen in the background.

Dawnnell rubbing the belly of a contented, happy pig on pasture.

Dawnnell milking her Jersey cows.

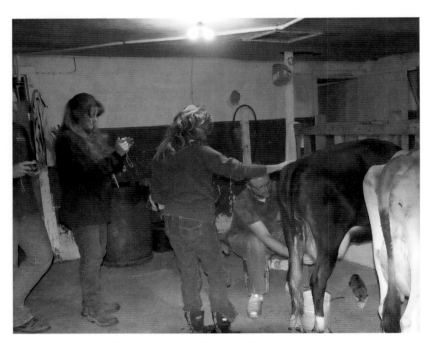

Teaching hand milking at one of Rockin H's on-farm events.

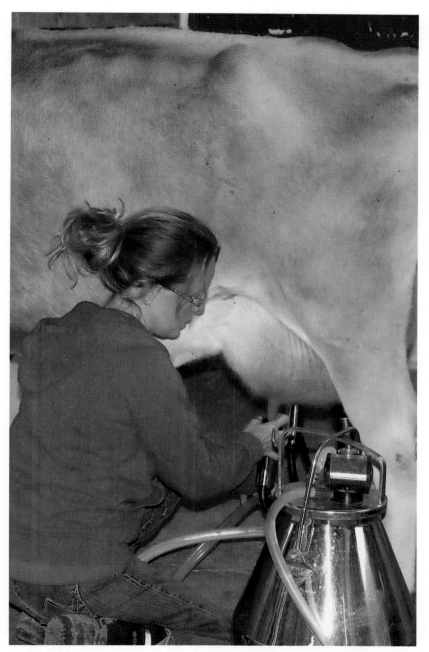

The farm has just one to six cows being milked at a time, so a simple bucket milker suffices. The milk is used for the family and sold on-farm. Milk sales make the dairy cow the most profitable animal on the farm.

Observing multi-species grazing — here sheep and cattle — is a beautiful thing.

A ewe is seen stripping fall berries.

Here the sheep are grazing ironweed, a nuisance plant for most farmers, but a delicacy for sheep and goats.

Sheep and cattle turned out onto a pasture together.

Sharing with other farmers and ranchers methods to be successful is part of the ranch's mission. Regular tours attract big crowds.

Cody teaching how to look at and discover the true nature of forages.

Papa Cody with future sixth-generation ranchers Isabel and Charlie.

Our first year retailing through a farmers market. The hard work pays off in direct feedback from consumers and capturing the full retail dollar.

Cody, Dawnnell and Taylor Holmes, with Brutus.

12
Holistic Systems for Stockmen

I WAS FIRST TURNED AWAY FROM THE WORD *HOLISTIC* when I heard it years ago because of my small-minded thinking. I am a happy Christian and love Jesus with all my heart. I will not criticize others who find happiness elsewhere, but I have little interest in learning of other religions, exotic or otherwise. My first thoughts when I heard the word *holistic* were that it had some sort of religious connotation. A lack of knowledge can be one's greatest obstacle if not corrected in due time.

I began reading Allan Savory's book *Holistic Management* quite a few years ago. Ever since then I find myself skimming that work several times each year. Other authors' words began to make more sense once I opened my mind to the thought that holism may have some credence. I have found that some farmers that appear to be most successful have been practicing in something of a holistic manner even though they may never have heard the word used before. Holistic is a very simple term to me.

It comes from the base root of the word *whole*. It is in this context that I attempt to describe the real meaning of the holistic system of farming that I believe in so adamantly.

Ranching and farming has become a key market for expert salesmen, marketing masters, and purveyors of products of all kinds. Modern agriculture is a multi-billion-dollar industry, and many companies are in business to get their piece of the pie. When our knowledge and skill levels are below an acceptable level in agriculture, we become a mark for these vultures. Our fathers and their fathers and their fathers before them have been farming amongst these sellers of products for way too many years for most of us to have learned any alternatives. Agricultural graduates are spit out from universities funded by some of the largest agribusiness corporations of modern time. Our statewide livestock organizations and their sister organizations have their hands in the pockets of these scavengers and promote high-input, low-thinking styles of agricultural production and have high-level agendas now spreading worldwide. Our politicians have even less real agricultural knowledge than our so-called farmers, and they have certainly been entertained by way of economic gain from their legalized "campaign contributors" with the result being a death sentence to innovation. So how is it that quality education from a holistic standpoint, that requires not great sums of cash or political influence, can ever prosper? It can only prosper if a lone farmer wants to turn his hobby farm into a profitable enterprise while at the same time raising healthy food the only way it can be produced. He will find that the holistic system is not touted on billboards or in headlines, but information is available for those who seek it.

Holistic systems for stockmen can be read about and taught through observation and practice. We learn that no single aspect of the ranch can be managed in isolation — as suggested by mainstream agriculture. The practice of raising bigger weaned calves year after year doesn't take into consideration that these bigger and bigger weaned heifers eventually make bigger and bigger cows. These big cows eventually become unproductive and consume more in feed and maintenance than the value of the calf they produce. This single-trait selection — or the lack of taking all things involved on the ranch into consideration when making changes — is the opposite of holistic farming systems.

In the early years of my ranching experience I began to watch one particular farm neighbor. He raised his family on a small cow/calf ranch with what income the ranch could provide. They appeared to have an average lifestyle from an economic stand-point. They lived like most the other families around except he did not have to go to work each day to support the ranch. The ranch supported the family. Bob had no farm machinery and spent no time during the busy hay time in May like everyone else working 16-hour days baling up hay to feed in winter. What little hay he fed in the winter was custom baled. I ranched next to Bob for only about seven years, and it was only the last few years that I began to see that he did not do what everyone else was doing. I moved on to a larger farm and began leasing larger and larger farms.

I began doing the things that I saw Bob doing on his ranch in my operation. Learning came very slow to me and I have no problem admitting my reluctance to education. But I was certain that machinery was a great evil and had no place in a livestock operation. I began grazing further and further into the winter without feeding hay. I also found that if I could allow the grass to grow kind of wild it would produce more forage in the long haul. This was hard for most people to accept. With the belief that our farms and ranches should resemble golf courses, this became a problem for most of my landlords.

I remember one particular landlord who was in his 90s and was very set in his ways. I was leasing about 1,600 acres from him at the time for my cow herd. He had sold all of his equipment except his 15-foot brush hog and 150-horsepower tractor. About the time I would get a few paddocks of grass knee high, he would chop it down to lawn height. I could not convince him of my need for that tall forage this winter. His holistic goal of his ranch was not the same as mine. My goal for that ranch was for it to produce as much forage as possible. He wanted it to look freshly mowed most of the time. He had made a lot of money from buying and selling farms and little to none from livestock production. He was good at what he was doing, but it was not really ranching. He also did a good job of keeping the tractor suppliers, feedstores, vets, and other input salesmen in business.

All of these challenges helped educate me in the holistic system of farming. Through my experiences, continued reading, and talking to good farm managers I began to formulate this system that once and for all could make livestock ranching profitable. By using the holistic systems approach, and not simply looking at production as an isolated event, my ranch began to turn around. After looking more closely through the holistic point of view, I realized I could not make this work the way I wanted it to on rented farms. In order for me to function holistically I would have to have complete control over all aspects of the ranch. This can only be done through ownership of the land. Holistic land planning is a multi-year program and short-term leases lead only to frustration and disappointment. This does not mean that farm leasing is not practical and necessary for the cash-limited rancher in the early stages of growth. But the long-term plan must include land ownership for success. With holistic systems in place, profits from a productive livestock operation can pay for the principle and interest costs of purchasing that ranch.

I designed the Ten Steps to Holistic Systems with ranch profit in mind. It encompasses over 35 years of personal, practical experience meshed with the insights and contributions from many different authors and farmers I have come across in as many years. As I list these steps try and visualize how you can incorporate these steps into your holistic plan on your farm or ranch.

Step 1

Determine who the decision makers are in the organization and utilize all their efforts to compile the group's holistic goals. This is a written document of one to three paragraphs stating the purpose and desires of the decision makers. This short letter format should be posted where it can be observed daily, such as on the door of the refrigerator with the valuable pictures of the decision maker's family. I believe Allan Savory best describes this by categorizing these goals into three distinct areas: quality of life, forms of production, and future resource base. You can break down your holistic goals into these three areas of how you see the future arriving. Remember to keep the lists short and precise. And only the decision makers make contributions in this area.

Under the heading of *Quality of Life* write out in just one or two sentences what you would like to get from the organization. List how you see the ranch contributing to your quality of life. This is not a list of weaning weights or cow numbers, but a list closely related to personal benefits.

Under the heading *Forms of Production* write out in what form you see the organization or ranch producing revenue, if revenue is part of the quality of life you seek. Again do not limit yourself to a certain breed of cow or chicken, but more generally species or types.

Under the heading *Future Resource Base* write out how you see your organization or ranch taking shape in the future. More specifically, describe where you would like to see it go or look like and what the resources or ranchland may look like once you get closer to where you want to be.

One of the main reasons I use this list of holistic goals is to verify that for each movement I make each day that that movement, decision or project is moving in the direction stated in these goals. If I have this list posted on the wall or the refrigerator I can easily question my task at hand to determine if what I am going to do today specifically gets me closer to where I want to be. The listed holistic goals are like a beacon in the night.

Step 2

Develop a methodology to help make informed decisions in the operation by starting with time management. This is best described by following a system of daily ranch management that is exemplified in the following Time Management Pyramid.

Time Management Pyramid

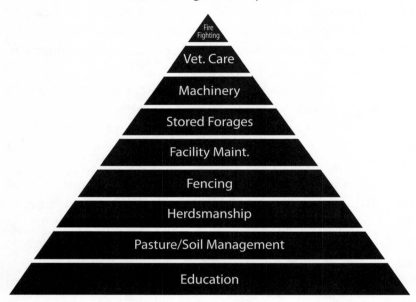

Many of us have the misconception that if we are not busy all the time at a high rate of speed that our time is being wasted. I urge you to conserve your time and eliminate all "busy time." We must have extended periods of the day to reflect on and observe the operation in order to make decisions which will lead us to our goals. This pyramid also demonstrates in picture form how a productive day might play out. If you start many days running around the ranch putting out fires and it's noontime before you can really get started on real projects, you are at the top of the pyramid with too much of your time. Or maybe you are spending enormous amounts of time riding around the ranch on the tractor compared to the time spent moving cattle from pasture to pasture, which will always be more productive and less expensive. It helps to remember that livestock have the ability to be productive on their own. They can graze, drink and move from one place to the next without your labor. We have to learn to get out of the way and let them do what they do best.

Step 3

Implement a system that can help you compare the economic viability of one enterprise on the ranch to another enterprise, whether one already in existence or one that is being considered. This is to help provide information so we can discern which enterprise is most likely to earn the greatest profit. Use the Enterprise Worksheet Forms (See appendix) to evaluate and monitor success. This is not to imply that all success comes from business profits, but one primary objective of most ranch operations should be net profit from operations.

These worksheets can be created using simple multi-column accountant's lined paper or with a computer program or spreadsheet. The concept is to isolate the income from each enterprise and allocate the expenses that apply to that enterprise. Generally we are talking about separation of animal species to determine if, for example, the beef cows are really making any money or whether it is the laying hens that are the most profitable. Isolating income sources and providing a check register system that categorizes expenses into enterprises or animal species is the best approach I have found to accomplish enterprise analysis.

Once we set aside fixed costs, which are the costs we have no matter what animals we choose to earn income from, we compare the variable costs associated to that income enterprise. In this analysis the fixed costs are generally first covered by the primary enterprise before any direct costs are compared. We then are able to attach the direct costs that actually apply to the specific species of animals or enterprise. This can also be a time to reflect on whether or not the chosen primary enterprise should remain or be discontinued. We must learn to be very objective during this phase. Our favorite animal or enterprise may have to be altered significantly or even dropped from the ranch altogether.

Step 4

Develop an understanding of the absolute necessity of solar collection and how it relates to ranch profitability. The only product a ranch really has to market is solar power. The tangible part that is transformed and provided to the customer is only the result of our efficiency at solar collection. Unlock this very simple process.

For most livestock businesses it is forage, or grass in general terms, that we are actually producing. We may be marketing our grasses through the sale of T-bones or cheese slices, but it is the quantity and quality of forages produced on the ranch that mainly determine our profitability. The production of forages on our ranch is directly dependent upon our efficiency at solar collection. The better we are at solar collection the higher our success will be.

I like to use the example of having a small 6-inch by 6-inch solar collector on top of your house and expecting to collect enough sunlight for everyone in the household to take a shower. The results would be improved tremendously if we replaced that little 6-inch by 6-inch solar collector with a solar panel that took up the entire rooftop. When we allow our grasses to grow to tall heights, rather than keeping them eaten down to the ground, our solar collector — forages — are multiplied in effectiveness manyfold. Just the same, when we fill in the empty spaces between plants and increase the density of our stands of forage in each paddock by high-stock-density grazing and animal impact, our solar collectors are increased. Creating a litterbank on top of the soil and a massive root system of healthy plants and organic matter below the surface, we are better able to collect the rainfall that once ran down the cattle trails into the creek and off the ranch. We can grow more forage when our neighbors are complaining about drought. We are actually harvesting sunlight, not forage or livestock.

Step 5

Unlock the hidden tools every stockman possesses on every ranch that will improve efficiencies and is absolutely critical for sustainability.

Grazing

Animal Impact

Rest

Soil Biology

We know that the more time a cow spends grazing and the less time she eats at the hay bunk, the lower our costs will be. As she grazes she expels about 27,000 lbs. of grass-growing nutrients each year directly on the paddock where it can be best utilized. All of this fertility is added at the cost of zero inputs.

The stomping of the litter from tall grasses into the top layer of soil — what we call animal impact — is part of the nutrient buildup done by the hooves of the bovine. From this point forward we can leave behind the concept of a fertilizer buggy. We can be more concerned with having 90 or more paddocks across the ranch so that we can get long rotations and long periods of rest between the times cattle enter those paddocks. It is these long periods of rest that are critical in producing tall forages that the grazing animal can work with to produce the desired animal-impact results.

Now the soil biology, our workers beneath the surface, can multiply and break down the fibrous material we call carbon first into organic matter, then humus, and provide the means to help sequester the nutrients plants require for even better solar collection. In considering the sun, rainfall and the atmosphere, it appears we have an almost perpetual motion machine on the ranch.

Step 6

Determine where the weakest link is in your operation and divert energy, money and effort to this problem first. Once this break in the chain is fixed, then and only then should we direct our efforts elsewhere. There is always just one *weakest* link at a time. This weakest link is the direct aspect of our operation that is keeping us from obtaining our listed holistic goals.

We may wrongly blame the small amount of rainfall as the reason we run out of grass each summer and have been forced to purchase expensive supplements for the livestock. In fact, the weak link lies in the fact we have not spent enough money on fencing so that we can do a better job of rotating cattle across the ranch allowing long periods of rest for each paddock. When the typical hot, dry summers arrive, our bare soils, short-rooted plants, and low organic matter in our soils thirst more than necessary. This reduces the soil's ability to hold moisture. It is clear that our lack of fencing in this case is our weakest link in this example. In this case, it may be easy to assume that all we need to do to get more grass is to spend more money on forage seed for the bare areas between plants. In fact, we do not even have enough moisture in our soils to support what roots exist now. A common mistake is to spend money, resources and labor on areas that are not the weakest link. It is more prudent to take the time and identify the single weakest link of today, make the corrections, and then when tomorrow arrives look for the weakest link for that specific time.

Step 7

Create a Financial Planning Model specifically for the operation. Utilize worksheets for entering data into a system that allows for monthly monitoring to compare planned objectives to actual activity.

Just as when we were using individual enterprise worksheets for analysis, we will have a recording system in place that encompasses the entire operation. This is best done using now affordable computer software with a little bit of training or can be done manually on handwritten spreadsheets. This year's results must be compared with last year's results as well as projections made before the season begins.

Step 8

Prepare a written plan to manage the land in a manner that does not contradict the holistic goals. This should be a one-page document that emphasizes the goals and practices referred to in the holistic goals.

By taking the time to describe, in light detail, our overall strategy, will help us better achieve our goals. Sometimes the actual words being written down and looked at closely will bring our shortfalls to the surface. This is no time for unbalanced egos.

Step 9

Prepare a total land grazing program covering January through December. This is a system of handling each and every square foot of land mass for each and every day of the year. Implement a fence and water design that utilizes:

Herd impact

Forward speed grazing

Rest

The herd impact of moving cattle from one paddock to the next on a daily basis will create a rest period of 90 days on each paddock once we have at least 91 individual paddocks in place. During the fast-growing times of the season like April and May for those of us in North America, we move cattle very quickly through as many paddocks as we can to get the benefits of forward speed grazing. If we wait until the forage is 6-inches tall in the early part of the growing season, the growth will overtake us too soon. These are some of the grazing practices that will allow us to eventually add more livestock to our operation without increasing costs.

Step 10

Implement a program designed to monitor both financial and land responses over time. Compare results frequently with the holistic goals and planning process and initiate a process for correction and re-planning.

A digital camera positioned within the same transects every year or every month for ecological planning can give us an idea of how our progress is working, for example, plant spacing.

Financial records comparing year-to-year results are critical for economics. Accurately kept records in binders representing each year of operation that are easily accessible will prove to be excellent resources for finding places in our operation that need correction.

These ten steps for initiating the holistic system on a livestock operation will require the continued use of advancement in education. You will recall this was on the large base and most important part of the time pyramid. As we increase our education in all that makes up this simple-to-manage but complex-by-design field called agriculture, our success will be enlightening. But studying and reading books such as this one, visiting other livestock operations, and attending progressive seminars and holistic system courses like I offer at my ranch each year are only part of this continued education which I am referring. These ideas can only come to fruition by spending the critical observation time down to the soil level, to implement changes where changes are demanded for better profits on the ranch. None of this can occur by remote control. And only those who properly respect ecology, animal behavior, and human interaction — particularly adaptation, soil biology, and the benefits of financial planning — will derive real satisfaction from the farm or ranch.

Appendix I
Sample Worksheets

Enterprise Analysis

	Gross Income
Minus	Fixed costs
Minus	Variable costs
Equals	Net Income

GI-FC-VC=NI

FIXED COSTS=The costs your operation would incur no matter what it produced

VARIABLE COSTS=The costs directly associated with a specific enterprise

PROFIT FARMS
INCOME STATEMENT
JANUARY 1 THRU APRIL 30 2004

INCOME

	SHEEP	5000	
	CATTLE	35000	
	MILK SALES	10000	
	TOTAL GROSS INCOME		50,000

FIXED COSTS	*LAND PAYMENT	15000	

VARIABLE COSTS	HAY	3000	
	GRAIN	1000	
	FUEL	5000	
	ELECTRICITY	1000	
	FERTILITY	5000	
	VET	1000	
	MILK COW PAYMENT	4000	
	TOTAL COSTS		35,000
NET INCOME			15,000

*Includes principle and interest

PROFIT FARMS
INCOME STATEMENT CATTLE
JANUARY 1 THRU APRIL 30 2004

CATTLE INCOME			35,000
FIXED COSTS	LAND	15,000	
VARIABLE COSTS			
	HAY	2,000	
	GRAIN	1,000	
	FUEL	4,000	
	FERTILITY	4,000	
	VET	<u>1,000</u>	
	TOTAL EXPENSES		<u>27,000</u>
NET INCOME			8,000

PROFIT FARMS
INCOME STATEMENT SHEEP
JANUARY 1 THRU APRIL 30 2004

SHEEP INCOME			5,000
FIXED COSTS	LAND	ALREADY COVERED	
VARIABLE COSTS			
	HAY	500	
	FUEL	500	
	FERTILITY	<u>500</u>	
	TOTAL EXPENSES		<u>1500</u>
NET INCOME			3,500

PROFIT FARMS
INCOME STATEMENT MILK
JANUARY 1 THRU APRIL 30 2004

MILK SALES			10,000
FIXED COSTS	LAND	ALREADY COVERED	
VARIABLE COSTS			
	HAY	500	
	FUEL	500	
	ELECTRICITY	1,000	
	FERTILITY	500	
	MILK COW PAY-MENT	4,000	
	TOTAL EXPENSES		6,500
NET INCOME			3,500

Appendix II
Resources

Organizations & Associations

ATTRA: National Sustainable Agriculture
    Information Service
P.O. Box 3838
Butte, MT 59702
Phone: 800-346-9140
Website: *www.attra.ncat.org*

Holistic Management International
1010 Tijeras Avenue NW
Albuquerque, NM 87102
Phone: 505-842-5252
E-mail: *hmi@holisticmanagement.org*
Website: *www.holisticmanagement.org*

Periodicals

Acres U.S.A.
P.O. Box 91299
Austin, TX 78709
Phone: 512-892-4400
Fax: 512-892-4448
E-mail: *info@acresusa.com*
Website: *www.acresusa.com*

The Stockman Grass Farmer
P.O. Box 2300
Ridgeland, MS 39158-9911
Phone: 601-853-1861
Phone: 800-748-9808
Fax: 601-853-8087
E-mail: *sgfsample@aol.com*
Website: *www.stockmangrassfarmer.net*

Graze
P.O. Box 48
Belleville, WI 53508
Phone: 608-455-3311
E-mail: *graze@grazeonline.com*
Website: *www.grazeonline.com*

Countryside & Small Stock Journal and *Sheep! Magazine*
145 Industrial Drive
Medford, WI 54451
Phone: 715-785-7979
Fax: 715-785-7414
E-mail: *csymag@tds.net*
Website: *www.countrysidemag.com*

Recommended Books

Malabar Farm
by Louis Bromfield
Ballantine Books, Inc.
101 Fifth Avenue, New York, NY 10003
Copyright 1947

The Clifton Park System of Farming
    and Laying Down Land to Grass
by Robert H. Elliot
Faber and Faber Limited
24 Russell Square, London, U.K.
Copyright 1898

Grass Productivity
by Andre Voisin
Island Press
1718 Connecticut Avenue NW, Ste. 300
Washington, D.C. 20009
Copyright 1959

Reproduction & Animal Health
by Charles Walters & Gearld Fry
Acres U.S.A.
P.O. Box 91299
Austin, TX 78735
Copyright 1993

Livestock Production
by Jan Bonsma
(out of print)

Holistic Management
by Allan Savory
Island Press
1718 Connecticut Avenue NW, Suite 300
Washington, DC 20009
Copyright 1988

Greener Pastures on Your Side of the Fence
by Bill Murphy
Arriba Publishing
213 Middle Road
Colchester, VT 05446
Copyright 1987

Weblogs

Holistic Systems for Stockmen
by Cody Holmes
www.holisticsystemsforstockmen.net

Allan's Blog
by Allan Nation
www.stockmangrassfarmer.net

Index

Savory, Allan, 21, 118, 165, 169
seedstock producer, 10
sheep, 128-129
soil tests, 32
soil, 110
statement, financial, 79-80
stock density, high, 25, 31
systems log of operations, 56

time management pyramid,
   170

tools, 57
Turner, Ted, 50

vetch, hairy, 94
Voisin, Andre, 86

Walmart, 63-64
water, 90, 97
wealth, 60
wormers, 42

Acres U.S.A. — books are just the beginning!

Farmers and gardeners around the world are learning to grow bountiful crops profitably—without risking their own health and destroying the fertility of the soil. *Acres U.S.A.* can show you how. If you want to be on the cutting edge of organic and sustainable growing technologies, techniques, markets, news, analysis and trends, look to *Acres U.S.A.* For 40 years, we've been the independent voice for eco-agriculture.

Each monthly issue is packed with practical, hands-on information you can put to work on your farm, bringing solutions to your most pressing problems. Get the advice consultants charge thousands for . . .

- Fertility management
- Non-chemical weed & insect control
- Specialty crops & marketing
- Grazing, composting, natural veterinary care
- Soil's link to human & animal health

For a free sample copy or to subscribe, visit us online at

www.acresusa.com

or call toll-free in the U.S. and Canada

1-800-355-5313

Outside U.S. & Canada call 512-892-4400
fax 512-892-4448 • info@acresusa.com